PACK UP AND SKETCH

Tom Robb

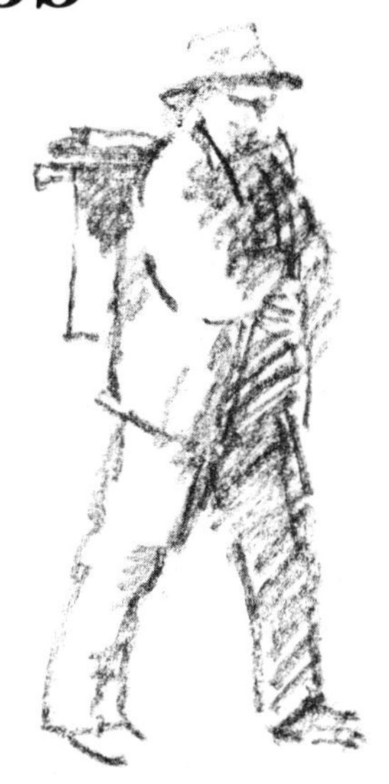

COLLINS

First published in 1986
by William Collins Sons & Co Ltd
London. Glasgow. Sydney
Auckland. Johannesburg

Designed and produced by PHOEBE PHILLIPS EDITIONS

British Library Cataloguing in Publication Data

Robb, Tom
Pack up and Sketch.
(Pack up and paint series)
1. Drawing
I. Title
741.2 NC710

ISBN 0-00-412127-9

ISBN 0 00 412128 7 (Watercolour)
0 00 412126 0 (Oils)
0 00 412127 9 (Pack Up & Sketch)

Printed and bound in Belgium by
Offset-Printing van den Bossche N.V.

Introduction

Drawing is the most direct act in any of the mediums we use. Pens and pencils are always available, and the hand really is quicker than the eye – quicker even than a computer. Outdoors, in a train or bus, sitting with a coffee or standing in a queue, scenes around your immediate environment become pictures within seconds.

Sketching and drawing are natural activities for every human being. We doodle by the phone, draw pictures on blank bits of diaries, scribble funny cartoons when we leave notes on the refrigerator door. Learning to harness these impulses, giving form and content to what we already do, can be one of the most satisfying aspects of art.

The *Pack Up and Paint* series is organized to help you make the most of every minute that you can spend. There are check lists for equipment when you make planned outings into unknown territory, and suggestions for the days when only the train journey to and from work will give you time to draw.

There are notes on the sort of individual problems that confront many artists in dealing with details, and a major project for experienced artists, to test appreciation and understanding.

There are tips on those emergencies which occur even in the best-regulated lives and colour shading codes to explain how pastels in particular can add to your finished work.

Above all, I hope this will be a *real* handbook, the extra hand that all artists could well use when occupied with pen and pad, not only to give practical aid, but to cast some light on the enjoyment of drawing and sketching outdoors.

Tom Robb

Contents

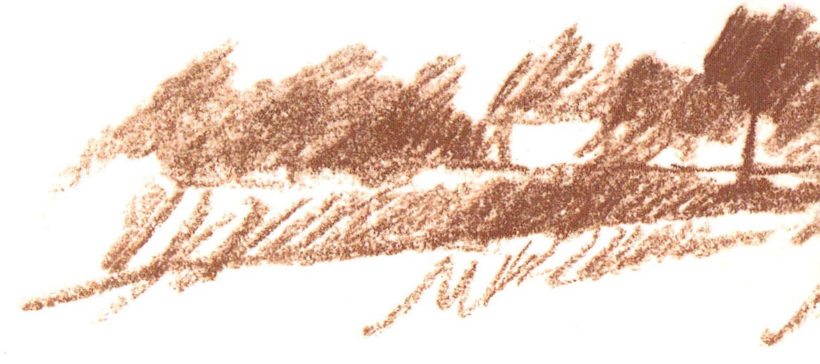

Why?

The two questions almost never asked, and certainly the hardest to answer: why are you packing up to go out and paint? Why are you spending time, money and effort to learn what to do and how to do it without knowing why you are doing it?

Through all the years that I have been a professional artist, a teacher and an adviser to countless students and would-be students of all ages, it has been startling to discover that these fundamental queries are missing from books, from classrooms, and even from conversations. Yet without a perceptive look into your own motives and needs, whatever you achieve will be less than you are capable of, and ultimately less rewarding.

So I have put down here the three basic approaches that anyone can make to art. It matters not at all which one you feel is right for you. It matters only that you understand what you choose, and why you may change in the future.

For someone who is looking for simple enjoyment, for heightened awareness of beauty through art, and for the sheer delight of being out in the open air with something interesting to do, my advice would be to ignore most of the detailed instructions. Take a pencil, a few felt-tip pens, a pad, a good lunch and a bottle of wine, and let the drawings happen. Use the information we give you to take the fuss out of colour mixing. At the end of the day you will be able to take pleasure home with you in the form of a sketch that is only for yourself – a memento of a magic afternoon, a reminder of an incredible sunset. That is rationale enough for any human being.

A second approach is usually the result of some years of learning, either on your own or in art classes. Having already attained a certain standard, you may be anxious to learn new ideas and perceptions as well as to increase your basic vocabulary of skills.

Your primary lesson would be an appreciation that all art is more than recording what you see. It is demanding intellectually and even physically. It is learning to take a structured approach so that you can get greater satisfaction out of discovering the artist's way of looking at the world. You need to ask yourself each time you set out what you want to achieve that day. Instead of throwing a few things in a bag the night before (and hoping you'll find a landscape in a bag when you get home) you should be sitting down and planning your trip, thinking about your ideas and how to programme yourself – the kind of 'psyching up' that is now so much a part of competitive sports. But this is not to win as such, but to force your precious time to work for you. These handbooks offer a ritual which can be used as a lens to get yourself into focus: looking over your equipment and setting it out; going through the five basics; trying to match some of the colour code mixtures for yourself. And each time you return from a trip with the landscape you intended to make, you will hang it up with a double satisfaction – both from the painting itself, and from knowing how you achieved it.

The third approach is one that is almost never mentioned, even to advanced students, and yet it is fundamental to the life of any artist. After you have been working for some time, you should ask yourself which you really enjoy: the act of creating a picture or the expression of yourself, which might be just as rewarding in another direction. Beyond this stage, painting is not necessarily enjoyable, and seldom entirely satisfying. It is demanding to a degree seldom recognized even in art schools.

If you want to be an artist in the full sense of the word, then it will permeate every part of your life, and everything you do. But the more you actually achieve, and the more you demand of yourself, the less you will probably enjoy the process!

This is perhaps the most serious commitment you can make and it should not be made lightly. Whether you are baking a cake or writing a letter to a friend or mowing the lawn, your mind will be partly (or even wholly) occupied with thinking about the texture of flour and the colour of pastry, the kind of pen you are using and the line the ink is making on the paper – or the difficulties of painting the thousand blades of grass with one wash. Read the letters of Cezanne, Van Gogh, Matisse; throughout their lives the greatest artists were always fighting their own limitations to create with their hands what they saw so clearly in their minds. The reward for most of us is in the effort, not the achievement.

The final project in each book has been chosen to provide a fillip for the more experienced artist; utilizing their disciplines will be another way of forcing yourself to recognize where you are going, and through which form of expression you want to travel.

A final word: none of these approaches is exclusive. The most casual Sunday painter will want to do something more now and then, the most dedicated professional must take time to remember how much fun sketching can be. Simply understanding what you need and want on any particular day will increase your chances of achievement and enjoyment a hundredfold.

Planning ahead

Here are the major factors which affect all of your trips outdoors, no matter when or where you go:

1 The time available
2 The place
3 The weather
4 The season
5 The purpose of the trip

Without settling down to go through these points, you will not be making the most of your time or your efforts. As you progress, it may become automatic, but even after years and years of teaching and painting, I find it useful to tick off the answers in my head while I'm preparing to go out.

1 The time available

Even the simplest of sketches will take a moment or two of preparation. There are occasions when an opportunity occurs that you could not have planned for – a youngster wearing the latest fashion, a curiously shaped house seen from the window of a bus – but most of the time there are so many choices that it makes sense to think about what you want to do most, and to settle down to concentrating on that particular drawing.

If you are an inveterate sketcher, a small pocket pad and a pencil or a stick of charcoal is all that you need. But you will of course be limited by the size of the paper and of the material.

The very ease and quickness of sketching can mean that you seldom give it a thought in advance, so make sure that you sometimes allow yourself more than the odd tea break. Plan to spend at least an afternoon and preferably a day every now and then to work on finished drawings and sketches.

Take a mixture of materials to give yourself a variety of line and tone and colours in the form of chalks or pastels or both. Treat the venture with the same serious intention that you would give to an oil painting excursion.

Time spent on improving and extending your sketching and drawing skills will be repaid in any form of painting that you are ever likely to undertake.

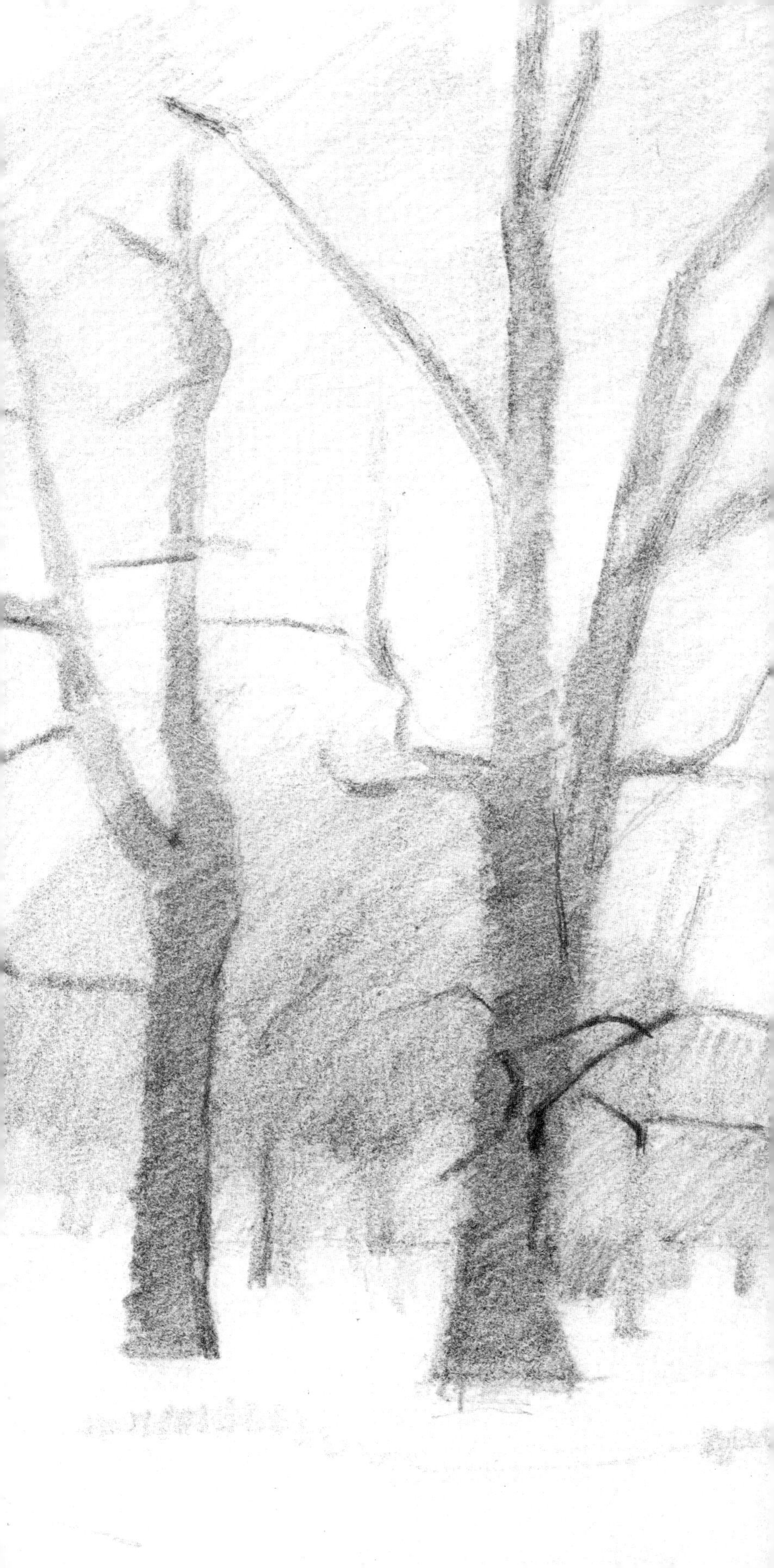

2 The place

The second factor in planning is your destination. Although this also is less fraught with difficulties for the sketcher than for the painter, there are still a few places and situations that require special care and consideration to ensure that you will be both comfortable and well-equipped.

Working on a slope is quite simple with pencils or chalk, but there are likely to be problems with ink washes. If you are headed for the high mountain ranges, then leave glass ink bottles behind; breaking them can be dangerous as well as messy. Transfer the ink to plastic cosmetic bottles with narrow necks. Fountain pens tend to work badly at altitude, and ballpoint pens don't always flow when they are held at an acute angle.

For a real sketching trip an easel is a great help. Although you can work for short periods holding your pad with one hand, it is tiring for any length of time, and it limits your mobility. You need to be able to look at drawings from various angles.

On slopes that are not too precipitous collapsible easels are extremely useful. Their telescopic legs balance on uneven ground. A three-legged stool to sit on has the same advantage.

Beaches and coastal areas are always popular venues. Here again, sketchers have a great advantage over painters in being free of the need for a flat mixing surface. An easel can be fairly firmly fixed in the sand, and a large plastic cushion or a solid-based stool makes a firm seat that doesn't sink unevenly.

A table easel can be handy for use in restaurants, pubs or cafés. Most restaurateurs think it an attraction to have an artist working in a corner, but you won't be welcome during their busiest hours. You are, however, likely to collect a crowd of onlookers no matter what time it is, except very early in the morning or late at night.

Buildings and streets provide particularly strong images for drawings of all kinds. Working early in the morning or after office hours will give you plenty of space, a reasonable amount of quiet and some striking views across the insides of buildings or looking through windows to the views outside.

Of course, for many people, landscapes are still the ultimate goal, and open fields and woodlands do indeed make ideal places for any artist to work. Here there are no particular restrictions on materials or medium. On the contrary, there is available a richness of natural materials which are seldom used and which yet can provide exciting textures and tones for your sketch book. This is one of the greatest assets of drawing – the chance to use the environment as part of your work.

I've suggested mixing clay or earth from the fields to make a background wash in the watercolour guide, but there are many more things that you can do. Here are a few hints to get started:

Chalk pieces make admirable substitutes for white chalk pencils, and add a certain rough quality of their own.

Lumps of soft rock give local feeling to the work, and burnt twigs or sticks were, after all, the first charcoal used for drawing images and they still work extremely well.

Nuts, green leaves, flower heads, sap from broken branches – rubbed on to the paper. These are all good materials in their own right, besides being there in an emergency when you've dropped your last bit of chalk off the edge of the cliff.

On the beach, seaweed and shells can be crushed up to form distinctive textures.

3 The weather

Once again, the sketch-book artist has an advantage over the watercolourist and the oil painter. No matter what the weather, there is a drawing medium which will work without any problems.

For extremes of weather, it is you who will need protecting just as much as your work, so make sure that you have a really waterproof coat; neutral density sunglasses (the type pilots use) to protect your eyes from sun or snow glare; a sun hat for milder days; and a pair of silk inner gloves to keep your hands warm even in the deepest snowstorm.

Really wet weather is the most problematical. It is difficult to draw, even with pencils – the paper gets wet and soggy even though the rain doesn't actually touch the surface. But do try to persevere with the occasional quick sketch in pen and ink; there is something magical about slanting rain and reflective surfaces.

Oil pastels work well in any kind of humid weather; they won't get crumbly and they keep their intensity of colour. Wax crayons are also useful additions to the wet-weather palette. In very cold weather, however, both oil pastels and wax crayons are difficult to handle: they become hard so that their marks are pale and scratchy, and pressing to intensify the colour will tear the paper.

Drawing in ink in the snow makes wonderful pictures of black and white starkness. However, it is likely that the ink may be actually lying on top of the paper in a frozen ribbon. So lay the finished drawing flat as soon as possible, and make sure that it is bone dry before you lift it again.

Light can create great problems in drawing. Try to work with the sun behind you, or at least to one side, to give the shadows and tone needed for everything except line drawings. Flat light, above all, is hard to cope with, since you have no colour tones with which to help define various parts of the scene. If there is no shadow whatsoever, pure tonal drawings can look almost meaningless. This is an occasion for putting pastels and coloured chalks to work to help give definition.

4 The season

With drawing there are two ranges of colour to be considered. Pen, pencil and charcoal create tones that can be used to suggest the textures and lines of seasonal changes, while pastels convey the traditional colours and shades of the seasons – leafy green for spring; darker, richer greens for summer; browns and reds for autumn; blues and greys for winter.

Spring

This is 'crisp' time; everything is light and clean. Use sharp 4H pencils, fine mapping pens, waterproof inks to make elegant, thin lines. Shadows come from an angle. Sharp charcoal pencils. Pastels: light blues, light ochres, soft pinks, flesh tones, Lime green.

Use smooth papers.

Summer

Pencils are deeper and thicker, HBs and Bs. The line is broader and stronger, the shadows more intense, often directly beneath the object, since the sun is in its zenith. Charcoal sticks and chalks. Use medium to broad nibs on your pens, to delineate the richer shadows as well as the line. Use red and blue inks in deep colours. Warm pastels in full-bodied Yellow ochre, reds, magentas, deep greens and Cobalt blues.

Slightly rougher papers than for the spring.

Autumn

This is the harvest of the year, rich and copious. Take 6B pencils, or thick charcoal pencils whose stumpy points you can use at an angle, after peeling off the protective paper. Use brown and deep red inks with broad nibs. Pastels and chalks: Burnt umber, Burnt sienna, Lamp black, Cerulean blue for the skies, Olive greens for foliage.

Rough, soft papers, almost like blotting paper, or waterleaf papers from Japan.

Winter

This is in some ways similar to spring, with sharp pencils in the H range, but on semi-rough paper, and with a reasonably black edge to the drawings. Charcoal pencils give you controllable blackness. Mapping pens again for fine lines, crisp snow crystals, icy flakes and peeling bark.

Pastels and chalks: grey, grey-browns, both warm and cold greys of all kinds, mauves, purples, Raw umber, Raw sienna, Ivory black.

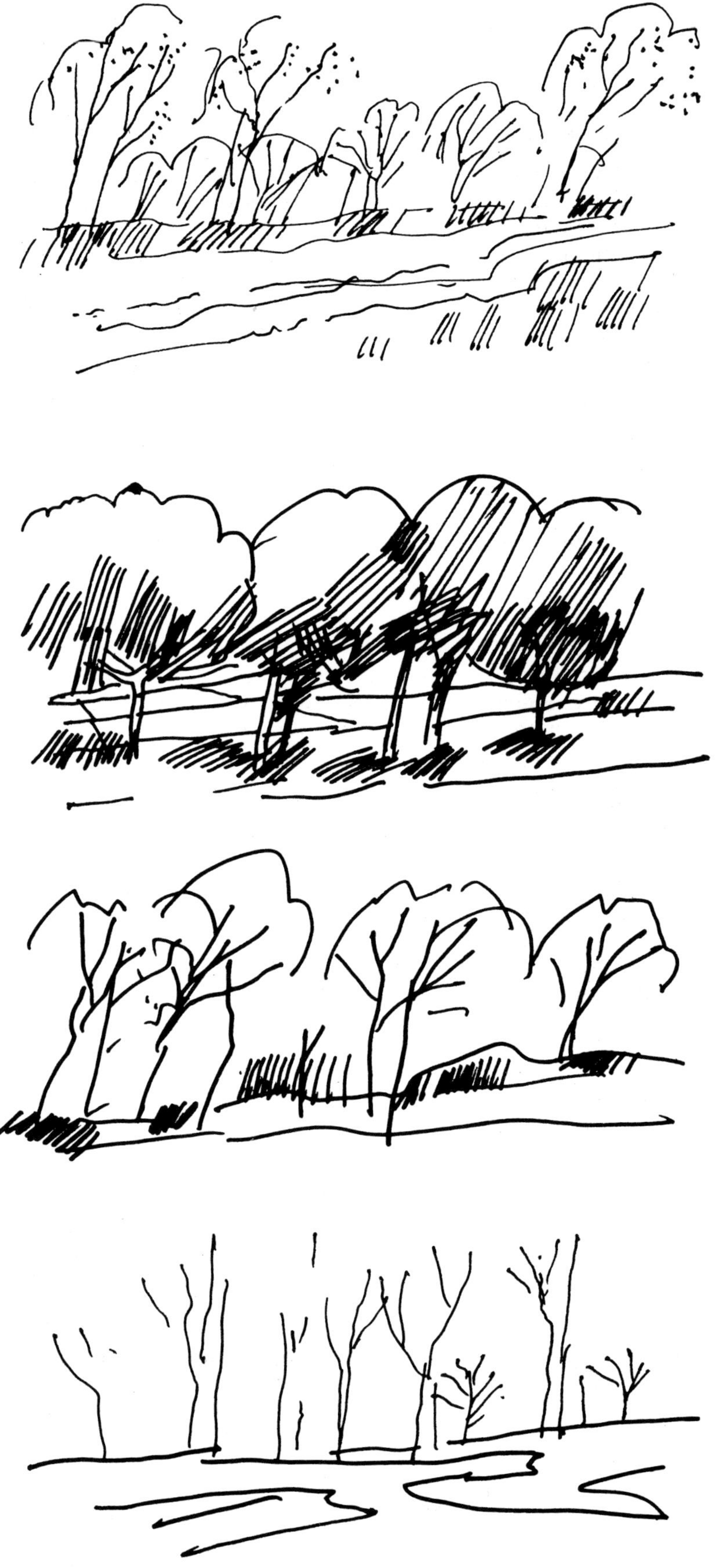

5 The purpose

There are interesting and vital differences between approaches to drawing and ideas and attitudes concerning painting in watercolours or oils.

For most teachers and students, drawing is considered to be essential to all the fine arts, fundamental as a discipline, and basic to an understanding of how to see. I cannot think of anyone who is a professional artist who has not made drawings at some time.

Yet we still tend to evaluate the result of this basic training, the drawing itself, as intrinsically inferior to a watercolour and, even more so, to an oil.

Perhaps the speed of drawing is its own worst enemy. Faster than Polaroid photography or any computer graphics, the artist's hand moves with a pace and deftness exceeded only by high-speed photography.

The analytical process in the artist's mind must be equal to this speed. Clear and definitive statements must be made unhesitatingly, as the image appears almost literally with a flick of the wrist.

This is the exciting aspect, the 'Look, it's magic!' quality which translates into the sheer delight of actually making something happen in a second.

But there is contemplative drawing, too. I sometimes spend a whole day working on one small detail – the infinite precision of a flower-head or the pattern of a rough-barked tree.

Working without the emotional crutch of colour gives a fine edge to the artist's eye, enforcing concentration on shape and tone, line and shadow.

So, since you have flexibility of technique at your command, your purpose for a given day may depend on the approach you choose to use – sketching at speed, or drawing with detailed deliberation. Whichever it is to be, make sure that you vary your choice of place for outings just as much as you would in seeking out new and exciting views for watercolours or for oils.

Having chosen your speed, so to speak, your second decision involves the two fundamental approaches to putting pencil to paper.

At its simplest, there are only two ways of drawing. One is to make an outline around objects; the other is to build up shadow and tone, thus creating an image without a firm edge.

Most drawing are dominated by one or the other method. Both have their grand masters, and each offers the artist a different way of looking at the world.

In a technical sense, starting with an outline is more difficult. Everything must fit within your fixed space. So it is often best to begin with the dominant masses – a group of trees, a large building – and work out from there.

A good exercise is to start work on several studies of the same view in tone with charcoal, in line with ink, and so on. Look at the differences between the elements in the view and assess how they are emerging on your paper. Is the foreground too dark in charcoal? Too light in line?

Experiment with using varying weights of line to create perspective as Van Gogh did: heavy broad strokes in the foreground, thinner lines as the picture recedes.

Then try to achieve the same effect with charcoal, and with inks, using broad edges as well as sharp points.

There are as many ways of drawing as there are artists. Each must find an individual vocabulary to use for this primary language of the fine arts.

Packing up to go out

Drawing and sketching can be so simple that it seems you need only put a pad and pencil in your pocket and go. This is fine, of course, for the kind of casual sketching you can, and should, do at every opportunity.

But drawing is also a primary artistic skill, and you should take as much time to prepare for your sketching trip as you would for a painting expedition. This may actually mean taking more with you than you think you are going to need.

Remember that your pens and pencils are valuable tools. Making sure that they are always kept in good condition both at home and while working outdoors is the mark of a serious artist.

Walking

Drawing is basically a one-handed activity, in the sense that you can use pencils, pastels and charcoal without any support system. You don't need a palette, a mixer or a fluid medium. For this reason, I seldom take an easel with me unless I intend to do several large, complicated drawings which will require a lot of moving back and forth.

I do take a good-sized pad if I can. Cartridge paper is fine for pencil and ink drawings, but if you enjoy using charcoal and pastel nothing works as well as really good, rough paper. This is harder to find in pads, but you can make your own by cutting three or four sheets into a convenient size, and tacking them to lightweight but firm backing board, or even stiff card.

Find a plastic brush tube that will hold your pencils, with a rolled bit of plastic over each of the tips. Pens can be easily protected in the same way.

To protect your chalks and pastels, wrap them in cling film or polythene bubble pack.

If you take ink and brushes, you must remember to wrap the bottles, and carry some water, too, since washes must be treated like watercolour.

A bit of clean rag or a sponge, a putty rubber and a sharp pocket knife for the pencils, and your pack is ready.

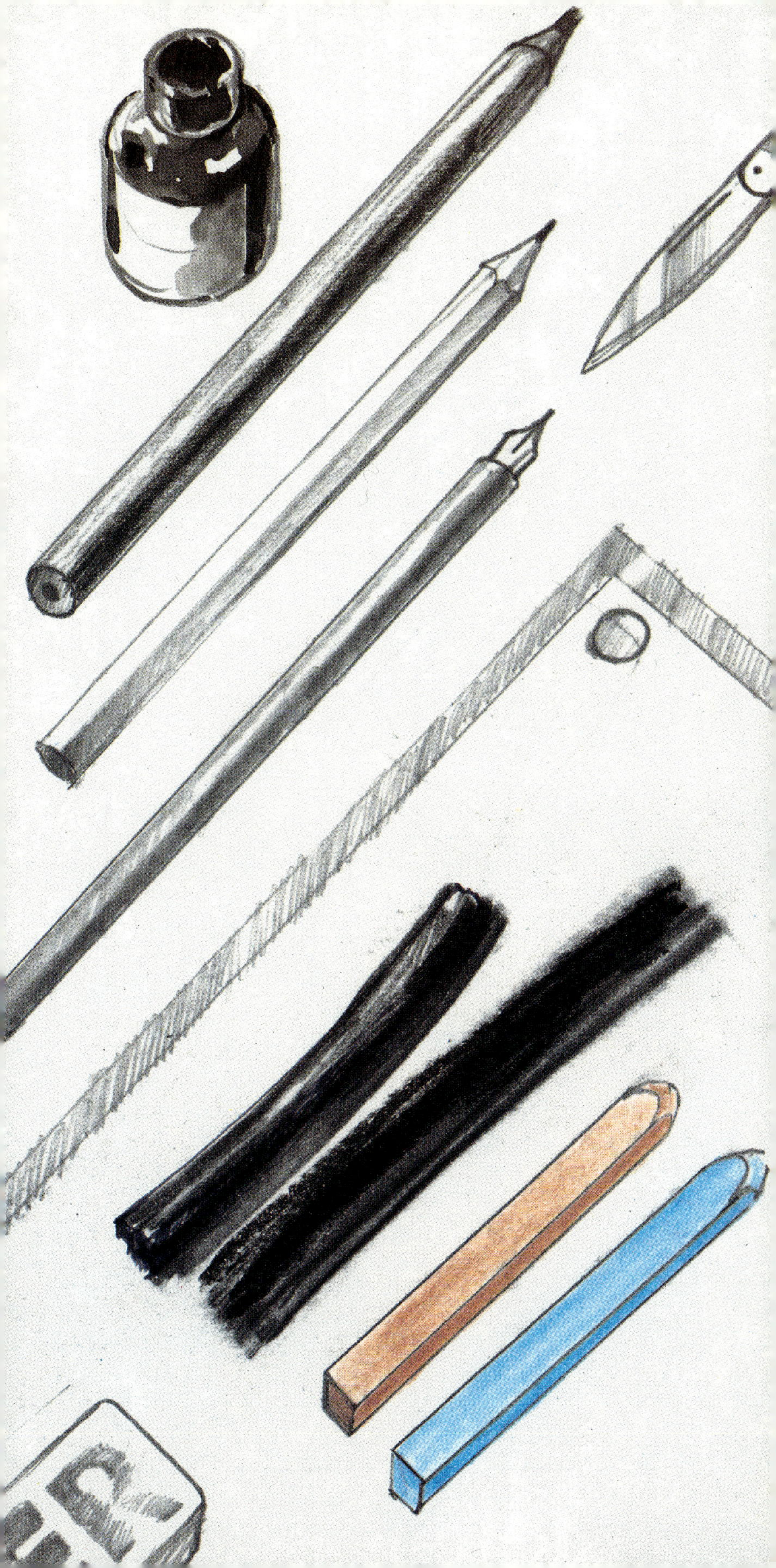

With transport

If you have a car or a van to carry your load, you can experiment with a number of different tools for different effects. But remember – you will probably have to carry your things to the place where you want to work, so don't overdo it.

Even if you prefer to draw with an easel, you are unlikely to want more than the usual lightweight model but for a long day's outing you might consider a combination chair and easel. It will save you from looking in vain for somewhere to sit in a busy market or an empty field. You may find, like me, that different mediums seem to have a curious psychological effect on whether you work best sitting or standing. While I always stand when I'm working in oil, I prefer to sit while I'm drawing.

You can afford to take many different kinds of paper. Make up your own pad from assorted sheets of rough and smooth stapled together on one side. Add a few new sheets each time, with unusual textures and finishes. Try coloured papers, especially if you are using charcoal or sepia conté crayons.

A cartridge pad permanently tucked into the back of your car, by the way, will mean that you'll never run out of something to draw on when there's a sudden inspirational opportunity.

Carry a variety of pencils, with their points protected by rolled tubes of polythene; a selection of brushes; two or three pens with different nibs, plus a number of bottles of ink, both waterproof and non-waterproof. Non-waterproof inks can be used for washes as well as for fine line drawings.

Pastels are quite fragile, but they and charcoal sticks usually come in neat boxes which you can carry just as they are. Conté crayons in black and *bistre* (their version of sepia) are a luxury, but they add a rich note to charcoal drawings and, like pastels, are generally used nowadays instead of chalks.

You'll also need a knife for sharpening your points; an eraser or putty rubber; a plastic water bottle; a few clean rags to wipe the brushes; a sponge – in its own plastic bag – to mop up any spills; and fixative in an aerosol tin. (In an emergency, you can use milk, as people did in wartime. The casein fixes the pigment onto the paper.)

Pack it all into a roomy biscuit tin, and you're away. But don't forget one last thing – yourself. Take along a vacuum flask of tea or coffee, a half-bottle of wine and a packet of sandwiches so that you don't have to pack up and find somewhere to eat just when you're getting nicely started.

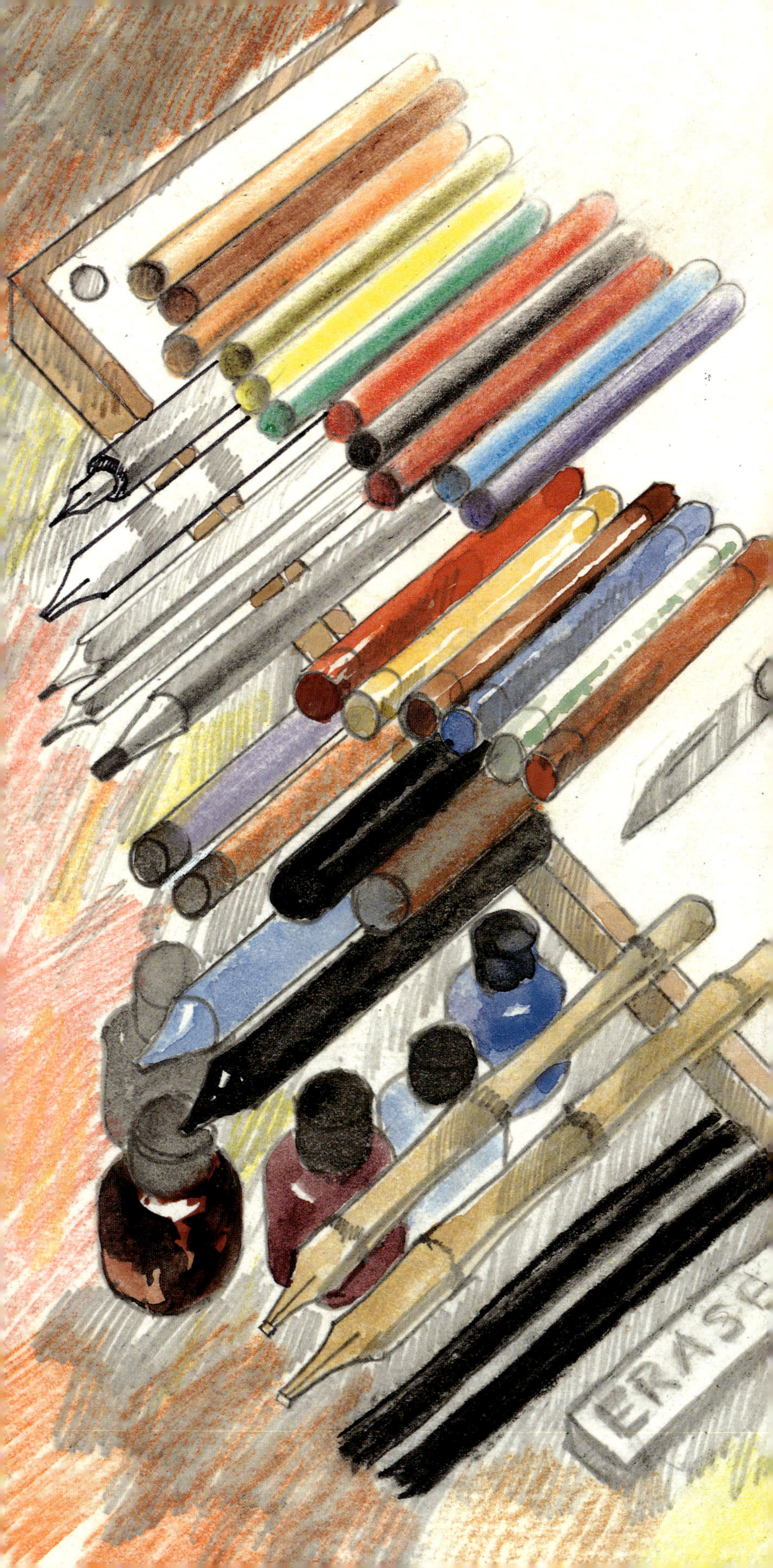

Pencils and pens

At its most basic, a pencil is a stick of wood enclosing a combination of graphite and clay in a central rod. The graphite mixture is the actual tool; the wood makes a convenient protective case for the fragile rod. Art students seldom realize how breakable a pencil is. Dropping one from a table can shatter the lead inside, and although it doesn't look broken, once you start sharpening, the pieces will simply fall out.

Pencil sharpeners are really not useful. Far better is a sharp knife, followed by a piece of sandpaper.

There are fifteen degrees of hardness in drawing pencils. Most artists use from 6H, the hardest, down to H, and from B to 6B, the softest. HB, at the centre of the range, is the most popular for all-round use, but it doesn't have much character for drawing. The 6B is a lovely pencil, soft and black, and I use it a great deal, together with a 2B and a 4H for contrast.

Pens come in a much wider variety of thickness, character and texture than do pencils. There are fine mapping pens so precise that you can draw every seed on a dandelion, and felt-tip pens thick enough to cover the paper with solid black.

Some stylus pens have a reservoir of ink which you can fill with cartridges. Most nib pens are used direct from the bottle.

Inks now come in such a wide range of colours that it is possible to draw almost any subject in any shade.

If you want to use washes for overall shadows, ordinary watercolour paint is probably as good as anything. It is better for your brushes than ink which makes them brittle and stiff, even if you keep cleaning them.

Cane pens

Cane pens, which have been used for thousands of years, are still practical today for outside drawing. They are cheap, effective and can be suited to your own requirements. You can make your own, in whatever widths you like, from a common bamboo plant. This grows wild in some places or can be grown in your garden.

Cut lengths of about eight inches (200mm) with a sharp knife. Carve these into the correct pen shape. (Always carve away from yourself!) Split the cane and cut the edges to the width required. Finally, cut off the end squarely to give a neat end to the nib.

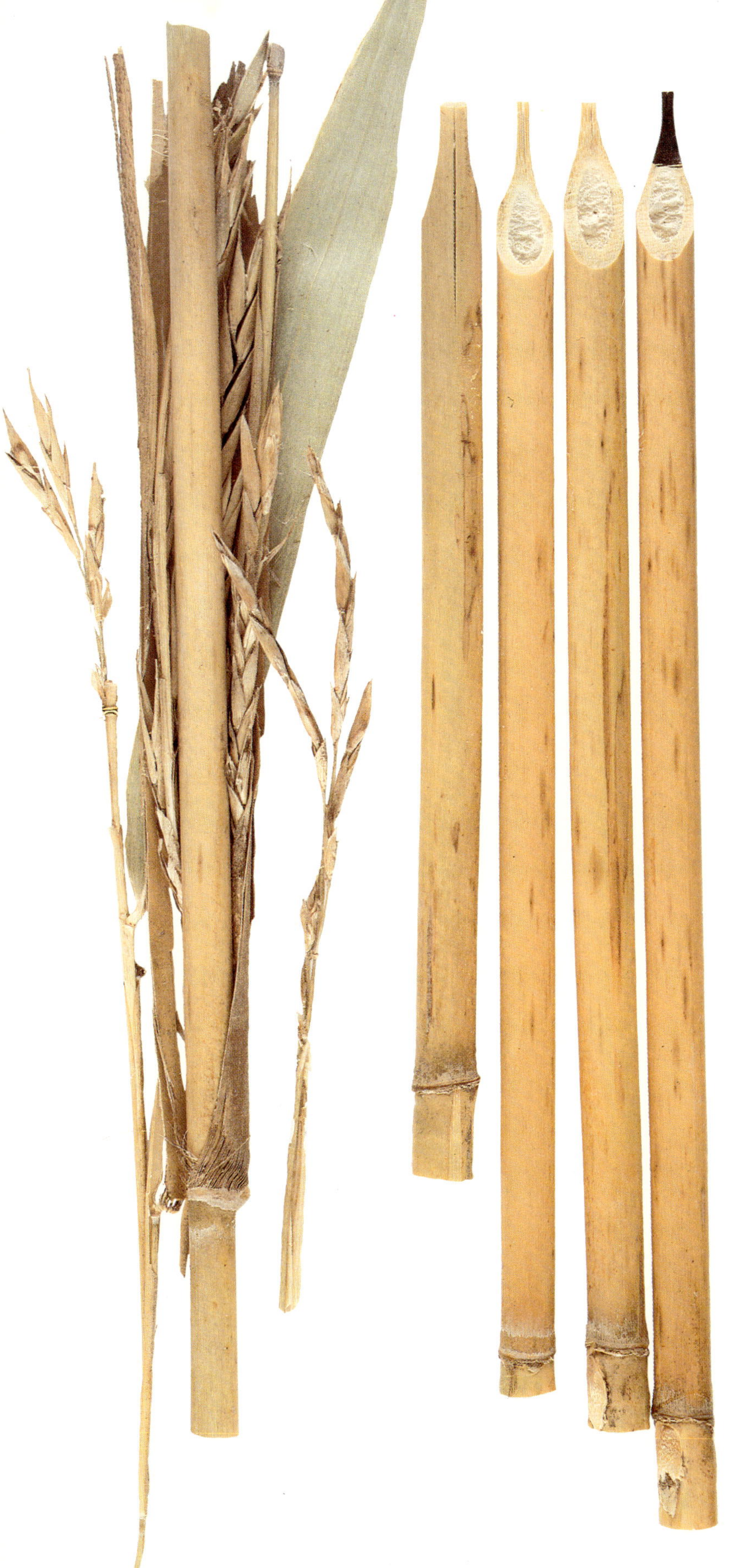

Pastels and chalks

Pastels are made of pigment mixed with various amalgams of chalks and gum. The dry paste has a tendency to flake off on rough paper, giving drawings a characteristic look of textured colour. Oil pastels, a fairly new product, give a more intense colour but with the same surface; they are supposed to need no fixing.

I enjoy drawing with pastel crayons of all kinds. They can also be used to create smooth-surfaced portraits and paintings that are difficult to distinguish from watercolour or gouache, but for outdoor work I suggest that you retain the distinctive texture and make use of it to add dimension to buildings and architecture of all kinds. The rough look seems to fit in well with brick, slate and stone finishes.

The seven basic colours you will need are shown opposite. They indicate just some of the possibilities that pastels offer. However, unlike oils or watercolours, pastels do not mix immediately: two layers will always look like two layers unless you spend time smudging and working the tones together. For that reason, some manufacturers provide a range of tones from 0 to 8 for each colour.

Because of their flaky surface, pastel drawings will need fixing when you get them home. For extra protection, fix them as soon as you have finished drawing. If it is windy or raining, take the drawings to a protected place before spraying them. When you are out in the country the boot of your car will make an admirable prop or easel while you do this. The easiest sprays to use are aerosol cans, and there are also simple blow-tube diffusers for use with liquid.

Chalks come in a variety of basic reds, blacks and whites. The classic sienna colours are the most popular, and conté sticks are usually used today in preference to old-fashioned chalk. I carry Burnt sienna, terra cotta and madder.

Charcoal is just what its name suggests, burnt wood. It comes in stick form, which is best used in a holder, and in pencils. The sticks are also in three thicknesses, from very thin to broad 'scene painter' chunks. Keep them in their boxes to avoid breakages. Like pastel drawings, charcoal ones need fixing.

Basic range

Pastels, unlike paints, do not have standard names for all the colours, and different manufacturers use various descriptions. Look for the right colour rather than the name.

Cadmium yellow
Cadmium orange
Yellow ochre
Poppy red

Vandyke brown
Viridian green
Cerulean blue

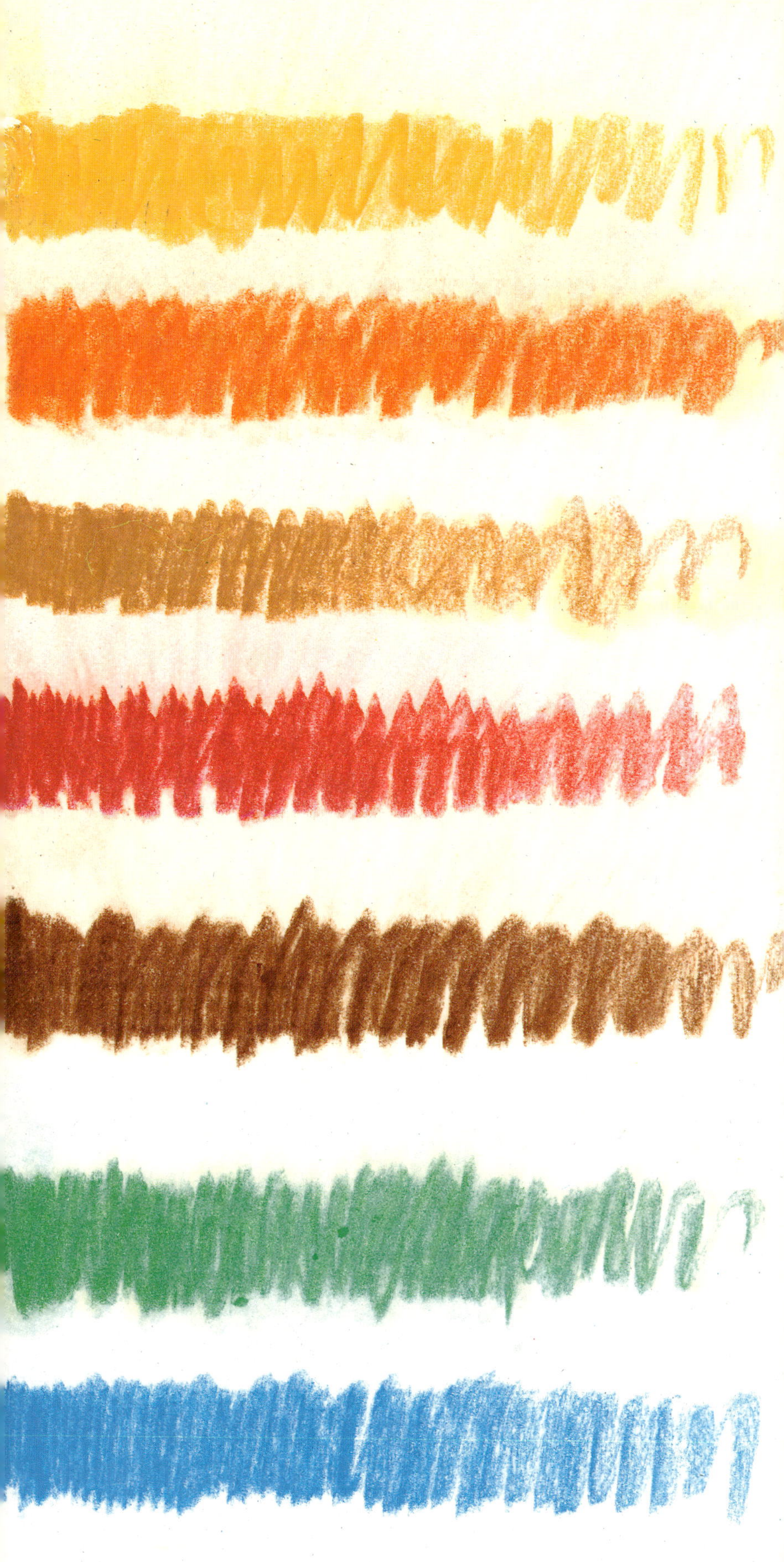

Papers

Although the standard sketching pad is adequate for casual outings, working with different papers and surfaces can be an education in itself.

The most obvious approach is to suit the subject to the surface. Corn in rough-textured hessian sacks should be drawn with a soft pencil on rough paper to look really convincing. In the same way, details of fine grass heads drawn on smooth paper with a mapping pen are particularly effective because the medium used to portray them in a sense imitates their image.

Unfortunately there are no pads of assorted papers, but you can make your own with sheets of different kinds cut to the same size, and lightly stapled together at one side. Then you will be prepared for any circumstance.

Make sure you include a few pieces of handmade paper, even though it is expensive. There is nothing quite like its surface for individual and striking effects with charcoal.

For regular use, reams of cheap newsprint are available in a good-sized stock. This paper yellows badly in time, but is invaluable for the odd outline or detail while you are travelling, and for making colour notes of landscapes and city scenes.

While coloured papers are fun to work on now and then, most are not really suited to outdoor sketching. Moreover, when you are first beginning to draw, they confuse the eye by distorting the colours and tints of the pastels and chalks you are applying. If you want to experiment, at least use a good paper that will give your pictures some texture. Ingres paper comes in at least 20 shades from pale sand to deep blue.

Heavy cartridge

Medium weight cartridge

Fine cartridge

Coated 'art paper'

Smooth M.G. or offset printing paper

Newsprint

Composition

A good composition is a pleasant balance of line, tone, shape and texture. Working without colour adds to the emphasis that is placed on these four elements when they are arranged on paper.

It may seem daunting to a beginner, but in fact we all spend our lives arranging things: our clothes, our rooms, our desks – even our futures.

There are a few basic rules to follow when you start making drawings outdoors.

Use the viewing frames in the front flap of the book to help your eye to isolate a picture in the larger landscape. Hold the page up in front of one eye and move the square or rectangle around as you would a camera, until you have a pleasant grouping within one of the frames. This is much easier than attempting to cram everything you can see onto one piece of paper.

Most drawings have a focal point somewhere to the side of the centre. This always gives a sense of balance far more effectively than if it were smack in the middle. The stronger the vertical focus, the more space you will need to give a horizontal balance.

You can see on the right four small drawings that I made of different views, as a preliminary to settling down to a finished sketch. Each had a different emphasis. The top relied on the colour of the fields. The second had a set of farm buildings, the third a great mass of trees and the fourth a sweep of the river. All would have made satisfactory pictures working in pencil, but I chose the second as I felt the spire added interest to the skyscape.

For a pen and ink drawing, the bottom sketch with its vanishing perspective might have been better, and in charcoal the third with its mass of heavy trees would have been striking.

So a picture is altered by your choice of medium as well as by your choice of composition. Never believe that the only way to use your imagination is to distort reality. Every choice is the result of your own creativity.

Experiment with drawing the same scene with one element missing. Take out the mass of trees, move the buildings to the far corner.

Try all kinds of combinations – charcoal and ink wash, pen and coloured pastels, pencils and wax crayons.

Small sketches are ideal for learning about which compositions work for you, and which are worth carrying on to finished drawings.

Making abstract montages from landscapes is also a lesson in composition, useful when bad weather keeps you indoors and you have to use your sketches for basic material.

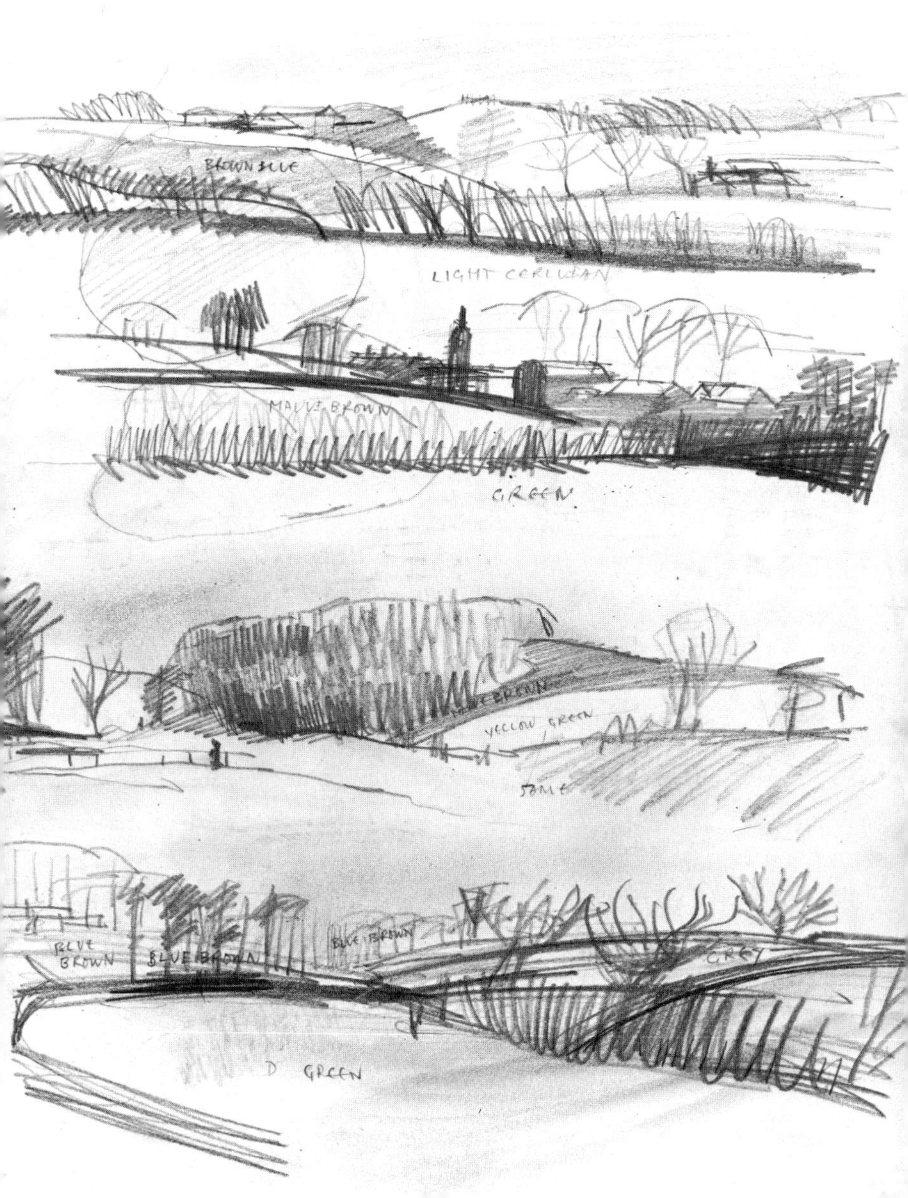

Choosing a view

Townscapes

In town, drawing and sketching is far easier than trying to cope with watercolour or oil. Although a portable easel is always an advantage, you won't need the rest of your equipment unless you are settling down for a day of sketches. Pick up your box of pencils, charcoal and so on and, with your easel, you are ready.

Since much of the excitement of drawing is in the speed, concentrate at least part of the time on making quick sketches of every figure that passes, people standing in the bus queue, cars, babies, buses, shops.

The exercise will quicken your mind as well as your hand. You will learn to see in an instant exactly what distinguishes one hat from another, one car from another. Give yourself time limits for each sketch. Start with five minutes, then gradually work down to a minute each.

You may have nothing more than an outline, or the set of a pair of shoulders, but that is enough.

Charcoal gives a good line, with enough definition.

Next, take the opposite approach. Find a building you like, and sit down to make a serious drawing – not an architectural drawing with all the perspective delineated, but a solid, detailed mass. Work from the windows and doors out to the edges.

Use pen and ink, then try pastels. Lay on the pastels in broad blocks, without trying to reproduce the exact colouring as you would with watercolour.

This sort of drawing can be particularly enjoyable if you work from a slight height, so that you can see roof and chimney shapes as well. The backs of high office buildings often overlook streets of small houses – an ideal subject, especially early in the morning.

You can see on the opposite page what an interesting, almost abstract, effect you can get by using pastels in rough blocks. Remember that the strokes you make with charcoal and pastels become part of the pattern of the drawing. The direction in which they are made shows very clearly, so keep them even and consistent.

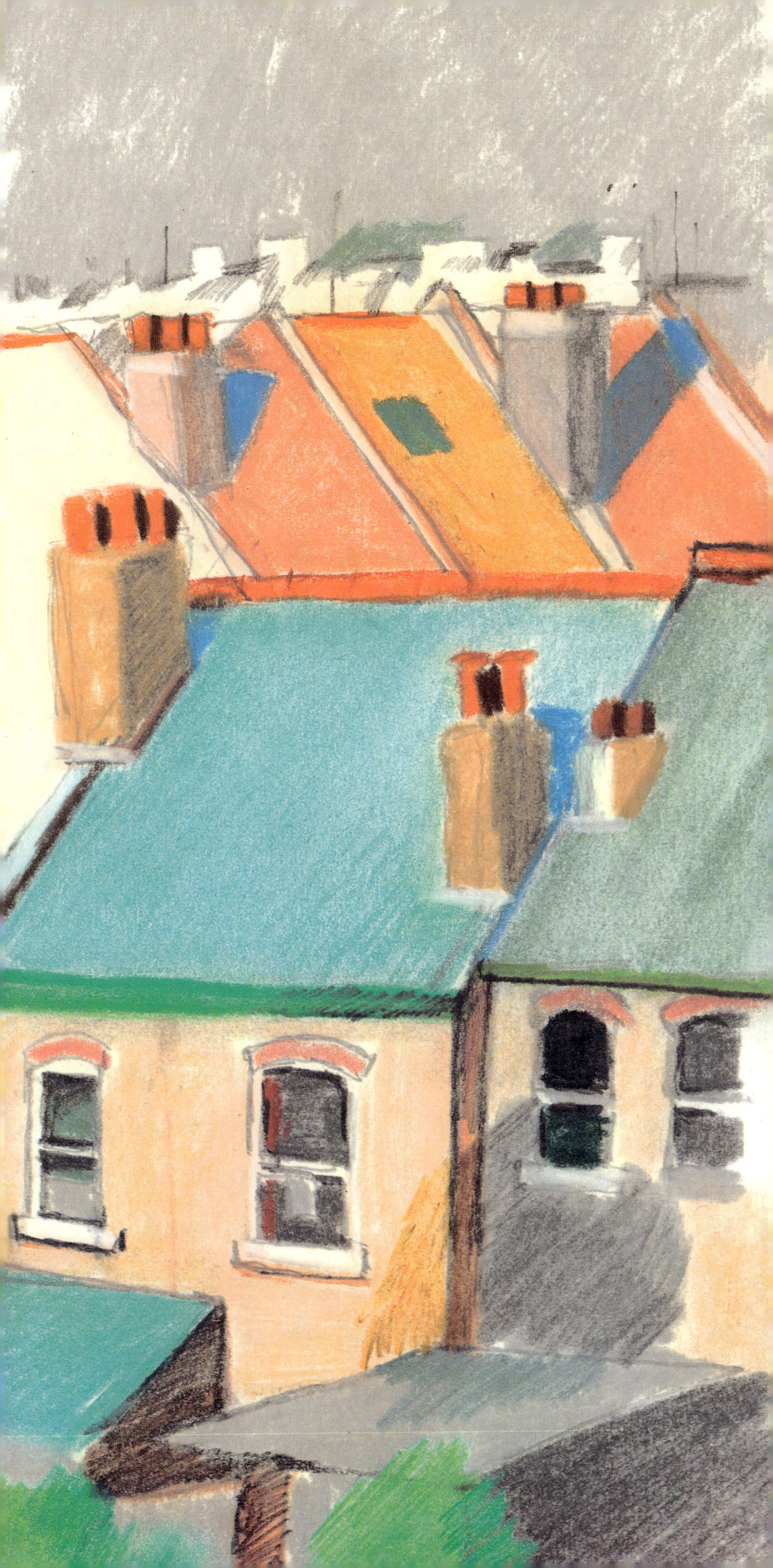

Countryside

Strangely enough, choosing somewhere to draw in the country can be much harder than it sounds. There are all sorts of obstacles along the road – hedges, barred gates, barbed-wire fences and wet ditches, with few flat pavements to provide a pleasant sketching spot.

Wide landscapes also offer less obvious material for a drawing than for a painting, since so much depends on colour balance, sweeps of various greens, crop textures in the fields, etc.

So my drawings in the country tend to concentrate on the intricacies of leaves, bark, and other details, or, more often than not, on country buildings. I love greenhouses – the lines of roof beams, benches and a twisted vine inside an empty greenhouse kept me busy for an entire weekend.

There are wonderful places to visit. Open-air farmyard auctions are a treasure house for the artist. Usually there is some sort of stand where you can be comfortable, and there will be endless views of animals and of people in crowds, staying conveniently in one place, unlike their hurrying townie friends.

Different places

Going out means really going out – away from your normal environment. Perhaps you have a special interest in landscape, in mountains or in nearby towns. Over the years you will naturally have concentrated on your favourite subject. But have you tried all the other things you can draw with a simple pencil and pad? Or any of them? The world is full of wonderful experiences.

Make a list for yourself of things to do. Tick off everything you have already done, and make sure that a least once a month you tick off something new!

- Hill country
- Flat valleys
- Woodlands and forests
- Mountain slopes
- Lakes and rivers
- Sandy beaches
- Rocky beaches
- Narrow city squares
- Wide city squares
- Small-town street scenes
- Airports
- Railway stations
- Small patios
- Market gardens
- Harbours, quays, marinas
- Boats, trains, planes
- Factories
- Sports scenes
- Churchyards
- Supermarkets

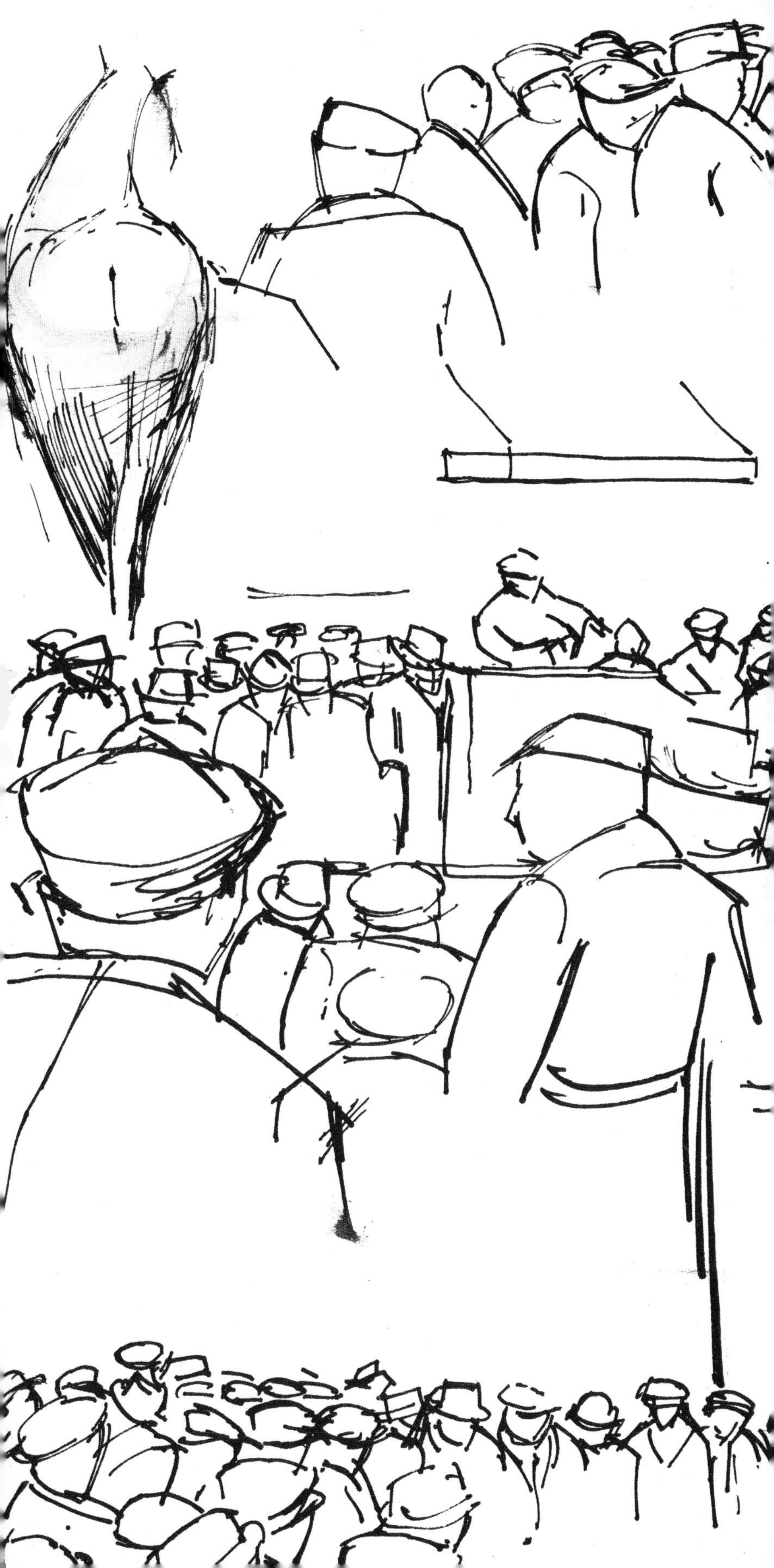

Details

Working on small details can be a special delight, even though the result may seem to be only part of a painting.

Pens, pencils and thin charcoal sticks are all ideal for learning about how something is constructed. You can look at an object over and over again, but not until you begin to draw the tiny details will your eye cease to be misled by distracting shapes and colours.

For any kind of detailed drawing, the medium you choose must be capable of a reasonably sharp point. A medium pencil is ideal. A fine-nibbed pen requires a little more dexterity but it will give you a sharp clear line that is perfect for mouldings, grille-work, lettering and so on.

Many drawing manuals provide a great deal of information on the formal rules of perspective. While this is useful in large and complicated drawings, it is not essential to artists who work well from observation. A good eye will develop naturally as you examine the world around you.

Once you can produce line drawings that seem right in proportion and shape, try the same drawings with added tone. Do not attempt to make detailed sketches with tone only, but add the tone, the shadows and so on to your line. This will give your details weight and dimension without destroying their crispness.

Never forget, though, that pencils can produce both line and tone. This detailed drawing of an ear of wheat was made from the freshly picked stem. I tacked it to the top of the paper and drew it just as it was.

One hour spent in observation will stay with you for many years, teaching you an incredible amount about a plant that you may never really have looked at before.

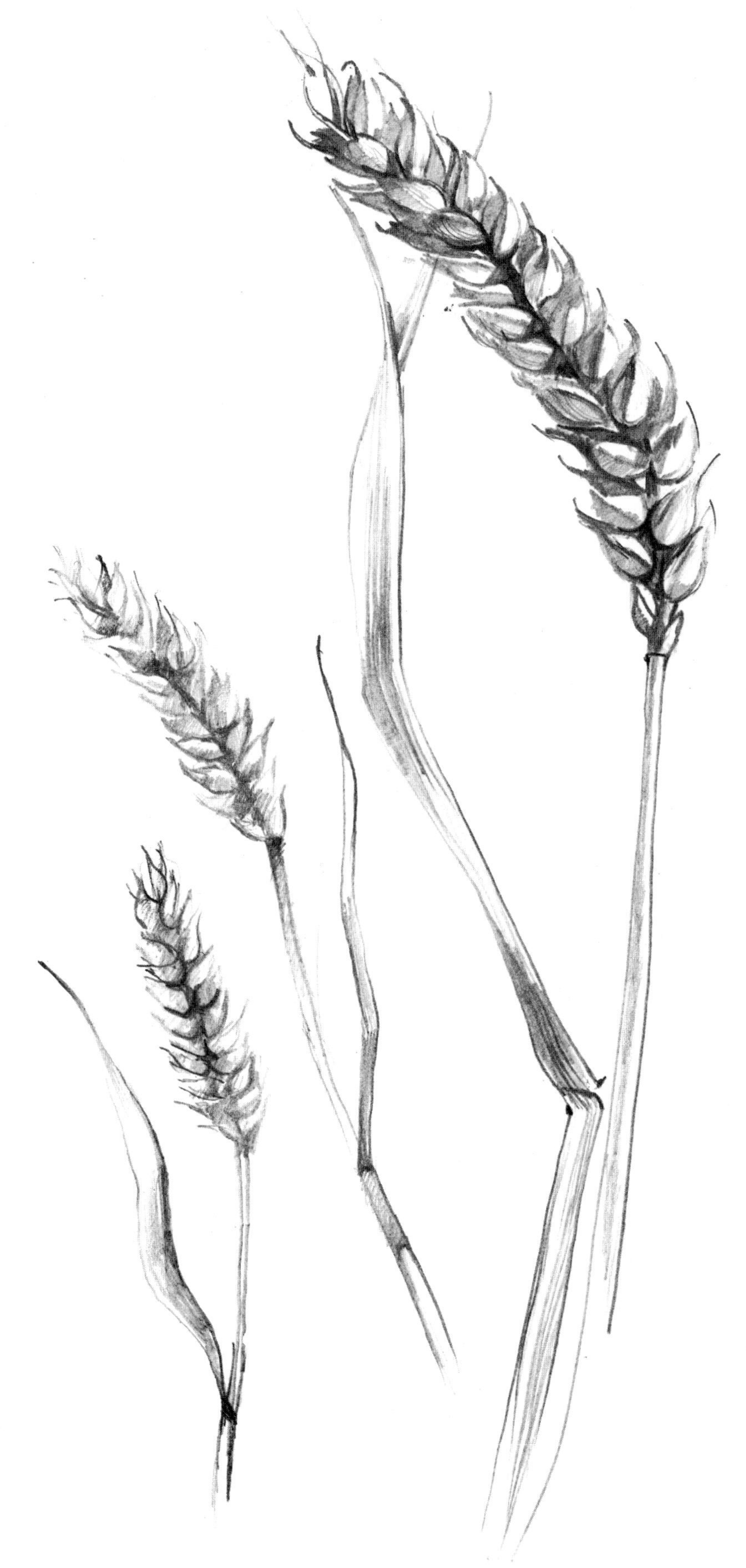

If all else fails . . .

There are days when it seems impossible to achieve any of your ideas in getting down to work. Your pen is leaking or the nib has broken; the box of charcoals has fallen into a flooded gutter and the pleasant seat you picked out for yourself in the park has been invaded by a squad of young mothers and their toddlers, surrounded by barking dogs and shopping bags.

Take heart, take a pencil and walk to the nearest tree. For naturalist and artist alike, any tree is an entire world in itself. Each leaf is the same, yet subtly different; each branch has its own shape and character, leading the eye into a unique pattern of interlacing twigs.

The fruit of the tree, in the form of buds, flowers, or nuts and seeds, can fill an entire sketch book, but just this once keep your vision in a narrow focus. Take a section of the bark of the tree somewhere around your eye height. Try to record faithfully everything you can see within the space of eight or nine inches.

Using a pencil is an excellent way of concentrating your mind on the lines and textures of what you are drawing. Without the use of colour or tone your work is much simpler and more direct.

Next time, pick a totally different tree so that the bark pattern will be quite unlike that of your first drawing. And the time after that, still another type. Gradually you will learn to recognize the features that make up the characteristic image of many varieties. Eventually you will be able to sketch a poplar, a cherry or a conifer, and put it in the most interesting place in your composition.

If you find that you enjoy this kind of precise work, pin all the bark drawings up on a wall near where you work at home. Let them become part of your everyday experience, so that the qualities that make up each drawing are imprinted in your mind.

Try the same trees using a different medium each time, at different times of the day; but keep always to black and white, or at least to monochrome colouring. Look at the patterns as if they were abstract designs for fabric, wallpaper or carpets. Imagine the same patterns on silk scarves, on a woven tie, as an inlaid piece of marquetry.

This is one way to develop an artist's eye – learning to see how the visual world is made up of patterns of all kinds, there for the taking, to use in your work in a hundred different ways.

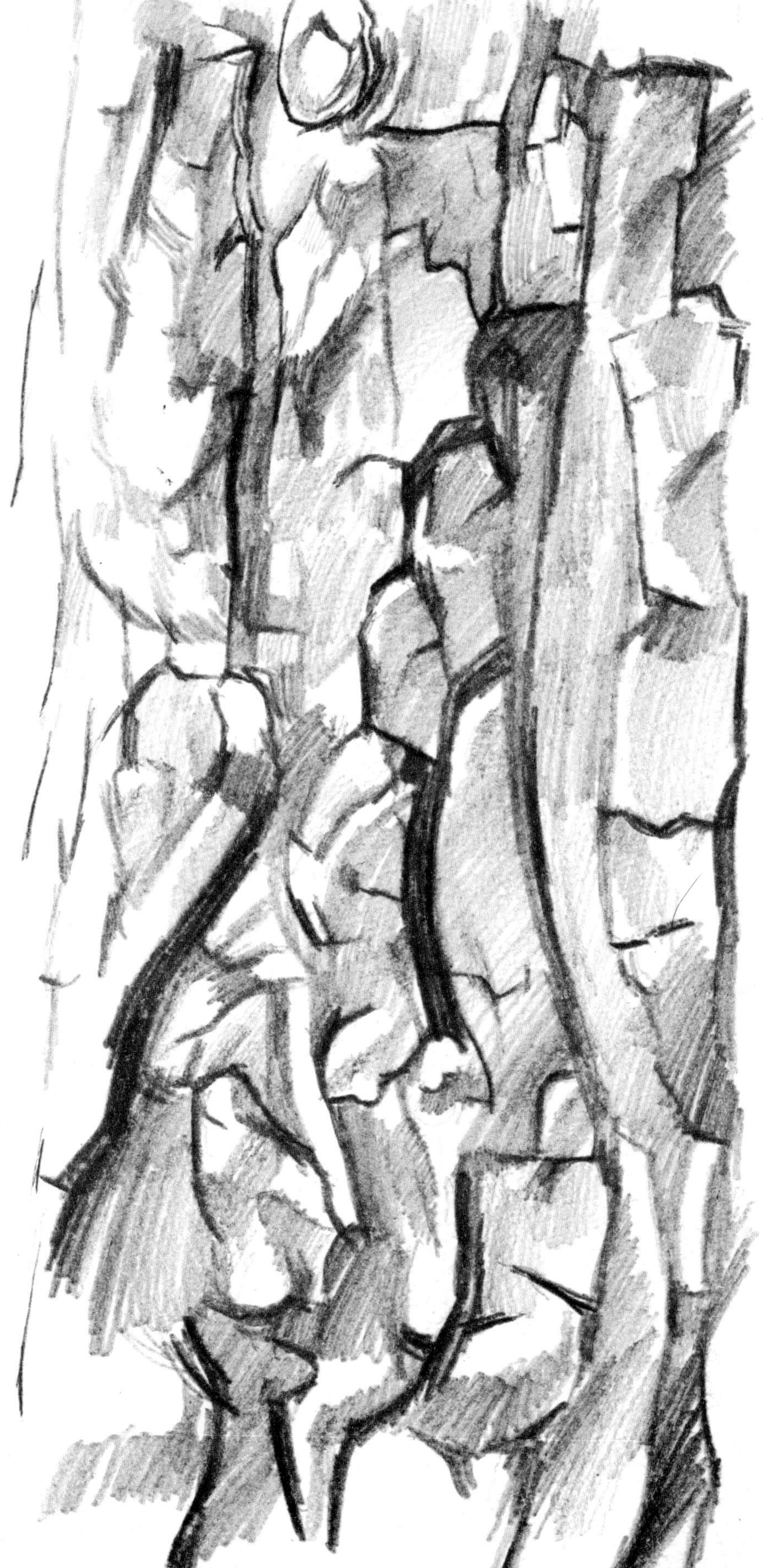

Special notes

People

Observation is the foundation of drawing, and, happily, it can be used every minute of the day. Keep a small sketching pad in your pocket or briefcase and learn to sit unselfconsciously in a corner while you record what is going on around you. This usually involves people, and most artists, even professionals, find this the daunting factor that keeps them from drawing as much as they should – and would otherwise want to.

To avoid embarrassment, don't imagine that you are drawing a portrait. If you were, you would have to concentrate on achieving some sort of 'likeness' to the person. Start with simply drawing shapes. Consider the whole figure as an outline (this is one case where it is a good idea to begin with an outline) and try to stress the three-dimensional aspect rather than the face.

Look at the way the arms are held, at the angle between the neck and the shoulders. It is often this – the set of the head – more than any other part of the body, that conveys a distinctive personality. It is also the one that alters least, no matter how the clothing changes.

Don't overwork a drawing like this. If it doesn't seem right, start again with a fresh outline. You'll see on the page opposite, taken from one of my sketch books, that there were plenty of false starts and different angles as I moved from one part of the outdoor café to another.

When you have covered the page, try another shape, another figure. Don't pick out too many details; use chairs, tables and surroundings only as part of the total shape.

Look for the angles which give depth and width – the creases and folds in a coat, the rakish tip of a hat brim, the squashed flatness of a cap.

Leave hands and feet as blocks of space rather than becoming involved in trying to make fingers and wrists and ankles move in the right direction. Later, work on only hands and feet, gloves and shoes.

The oldest trick is to draw your own hands and feet, but that isn't as easy as it sounds, since your foreshortened view will never give you the accurate observation that you need. Look in the mirror for a better perspective.

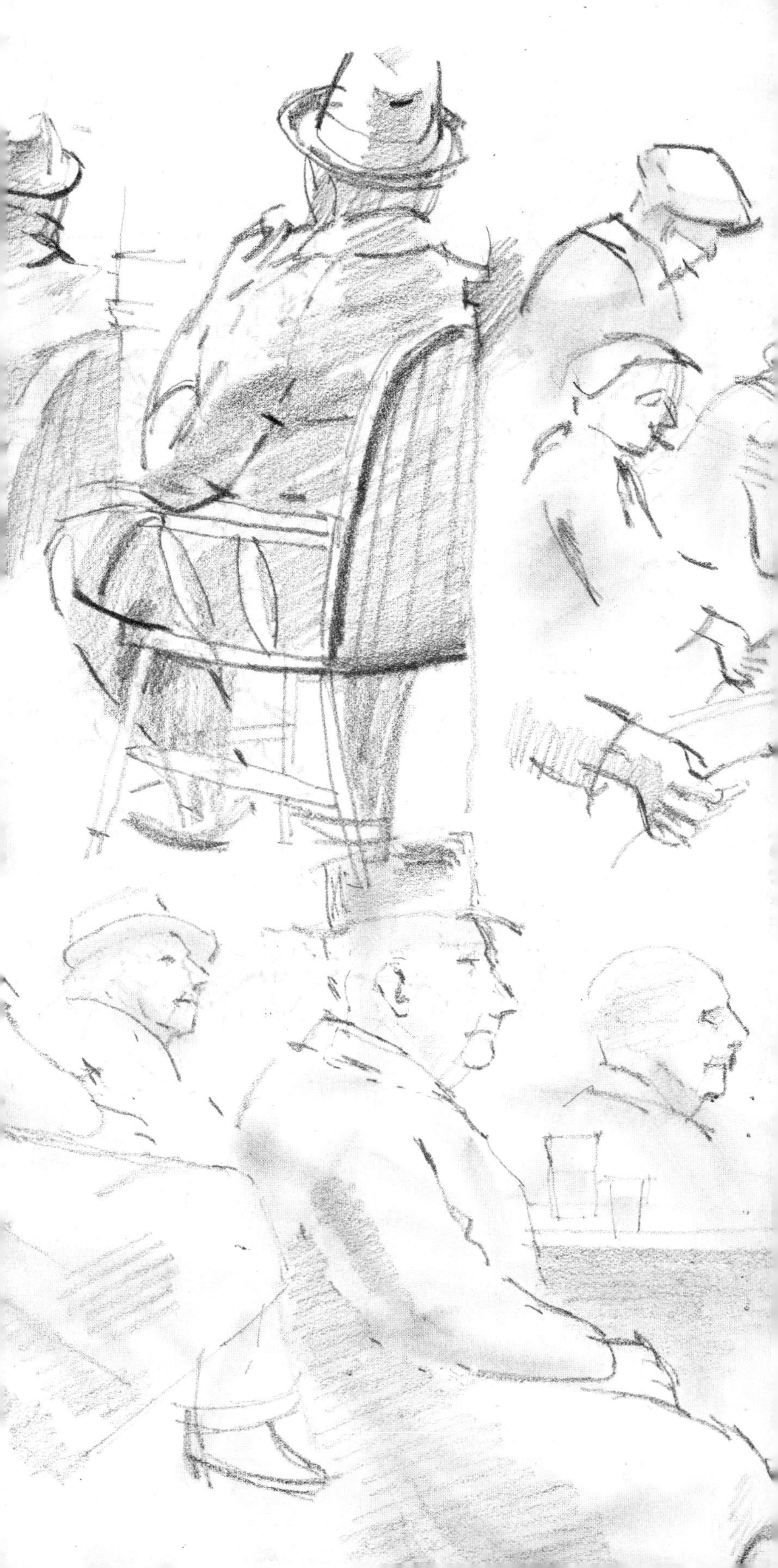

Buildings

Since so much drawing and sketching is done in town, the shape and form of a building is likely to occupy one of the most important spaces in any picture.

Begin as you would for a watercolour; that is, don't draw an outline first, but work from the windows and doors outwards. In this way your proportions are likely to be right the first time.

Look particularly carefully at the spaces between the windows. This will immediately set the correct architectural style. Old cottages, for example, seldom have matching windows; they were added here and there as the need occurred, often in quite different sizes and even with different kinds of glass panes.

By the time our modern cities were developing in the early Victorian period, building had become so standardized that entire sections were constructed at the same time, each house just like its neighbour.

This is still true today. The detail below shows a modern estate with its rows of identical houses. No doubt that is how the pair of terraced houses in the pastel sketch opposite looked when they were first built, but by now they have acquired some highly individual touches.

These are the character-filled details that give such a terrace its charm and sense of a particular community – don't ignore them when you start to sketch.

Look for the variations in brick colouring, the slightly dropped angle of the wooden sills, the door frames, the chimney pots.

Pastels are ideal for drawing brick and stone patterns. In a pen drawing, you might add a few patches of brickwork here and there over a wash.

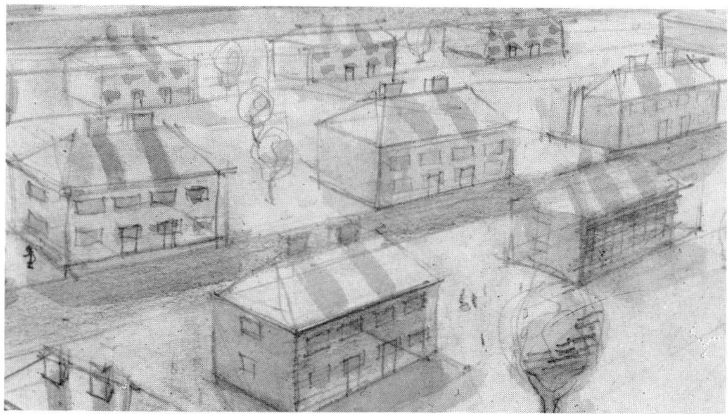

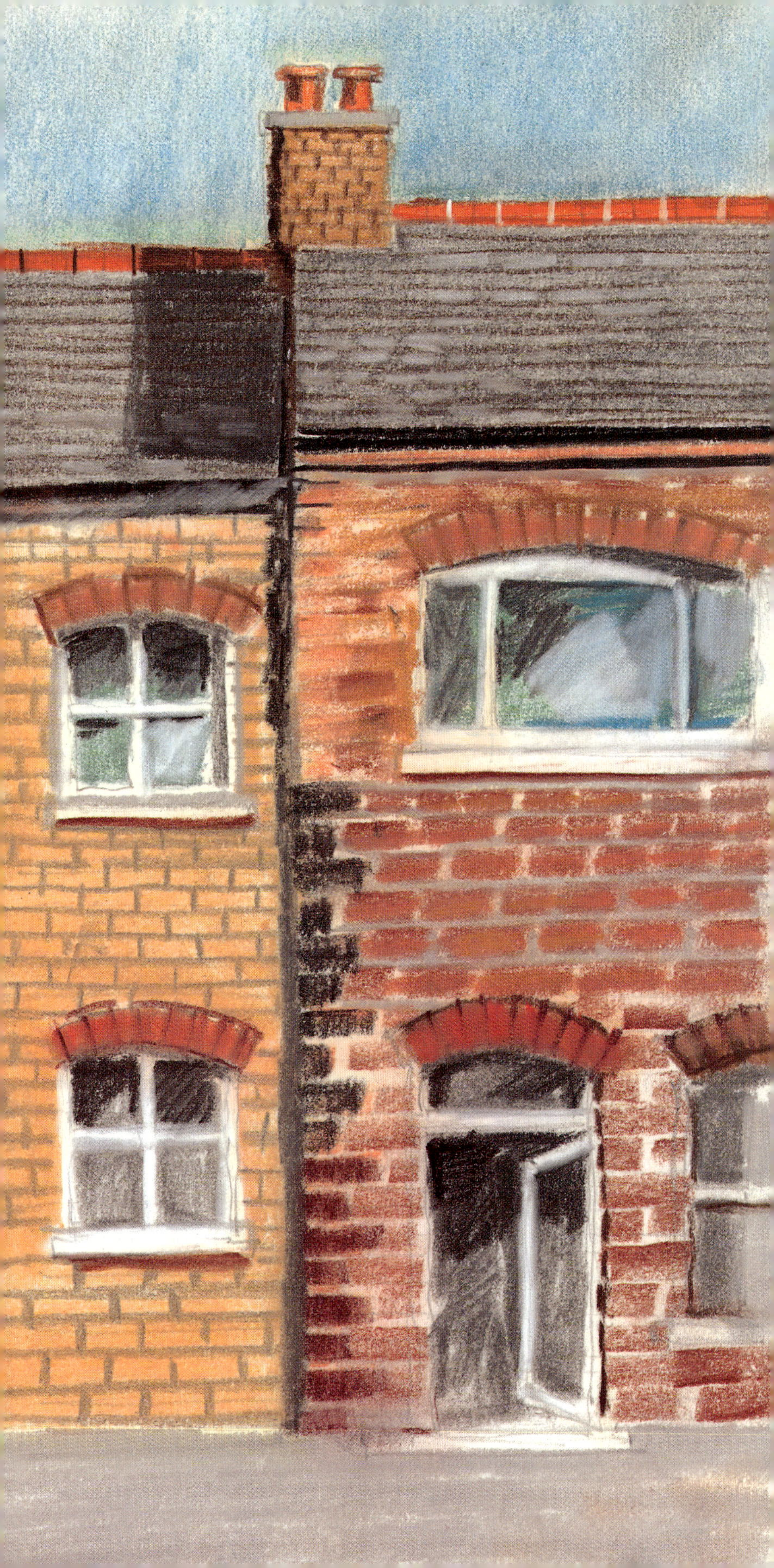

Lettering

One way of creating atmosphere is to draw in the lettering which always makes such a strong impact in a street scene. Even at its most obvious – being in the right language – lettering conveys an image. Think of any drawing of a row of shops where the word *boulangerie* is sketched in; immediately you know where you are, and often what period you are in, simply from the type of lettering.

Pens and pencils do the job best. Charcoal tends to smudge and to thicken too much.

Block out the space the lettering is to occupy and, with a light pencil, mark in the words, making sure that you fill the space. Then define them with firmer strokes or, better still, with a pen.

If there are different kinds of lettering in the scene, so much the better. You can have fun with three-dimensional signs, hoardings, neon script and so on.

Think of how products are associated with a particular form of lettering (Coca-Cola, for example) and how much city scenes, especially at night, depend on the signs to make them vivid and instantly recognizable.

The idea is to capture the style of the letters rather than to convey specific detail. Look for the little extras that distinguish one kind of type from another: the curly serifs on some classic styles, the effect of shadow on sculpted letters, the combinations that make up well-known logos.

As you look more carefully around you, your sensitivity to modern graphics will increase along with your skill, and you will be able to judge the way designers and signwriters have used the mediums at their disposal.

You can start a notebook of the international 'image' signs that are now seen everywhere, and which depend on easily identifiable pictures rather than on language – motorway and rest-room signs, concert hall and shopping-centre directions, traffic indicators. Ask yourself whether they work, and why you think they might be better, clearer or even more universal.

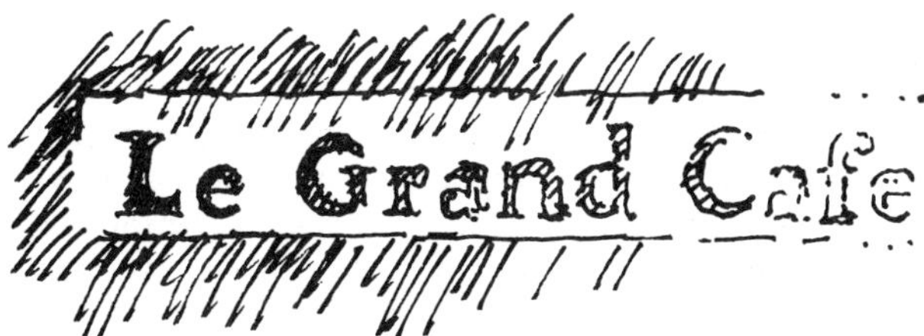
Le Grand Cafe

The Sweet Onion

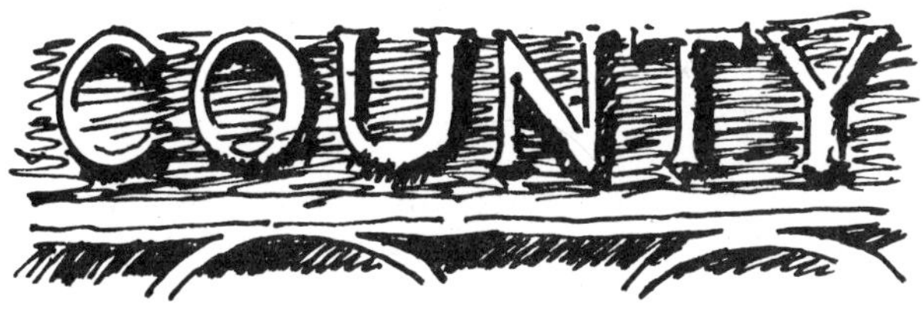
COUNTY

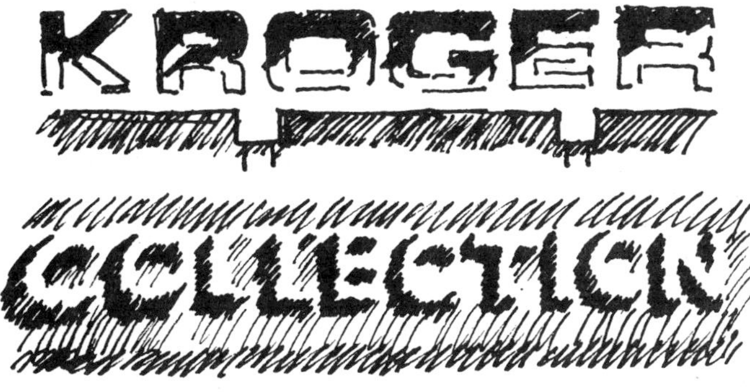
KROGER
COLLECTION

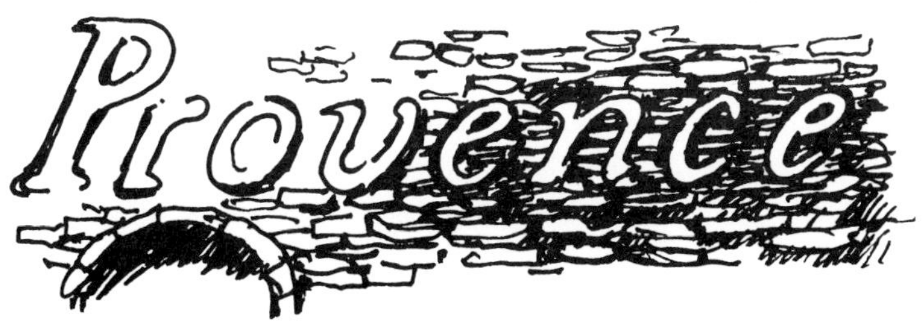
Provence

Boats

I have to admit a passionate preference for drawing boats. I get away whenever I can to sail in races or simply up and down rivers and coastal waters, and an essential part of my gear is always a drawing pad.

Boats provide a wonderful multiplicity of choices for artists. To begin with, they are intrinsically graceful with the lines of the hull, sails and mast creating a natural balance between the horizontal and the vertical. Add billowing sails, the glitter of brass in the sunlight and the smudge of rich red brown from the wooden decks and I think anyone would reach at once for their drawing materials. There are wonderful surfaces, too – planked and whitened wood, reflections from portholes and metalwork, rough canvas and ribbed rope patterns. All provide material for weeks of drawing and sketching.

Night-time has its own particular attraction for artists, and nowhere is it more exciting than in a harbour or marina, where the daytime bustle and glut of colours is transformed into a ghostly forest of creaking masts, almost unseen in the darkness but making their presence felt as long lines pointing to the sky.

In the charcoal drawing opposite I was exploring the effect of drawing around the light rather than drawing the boats themselves. The rich blackness of charcoal pencil is ideal for creating the impression of darkness, contrasting with the white spaces depicting pools of light. A few quick strokes for the masts and the stooping figure of a sailor, some squiggles to indicate reflections on the water and the scene is finished.

Never try to overwork a picture like this. It depends on spontaneity and freshness for effect. If you are unhappy about something, start again. It will be quicker in the longer run, and more satisfactory.

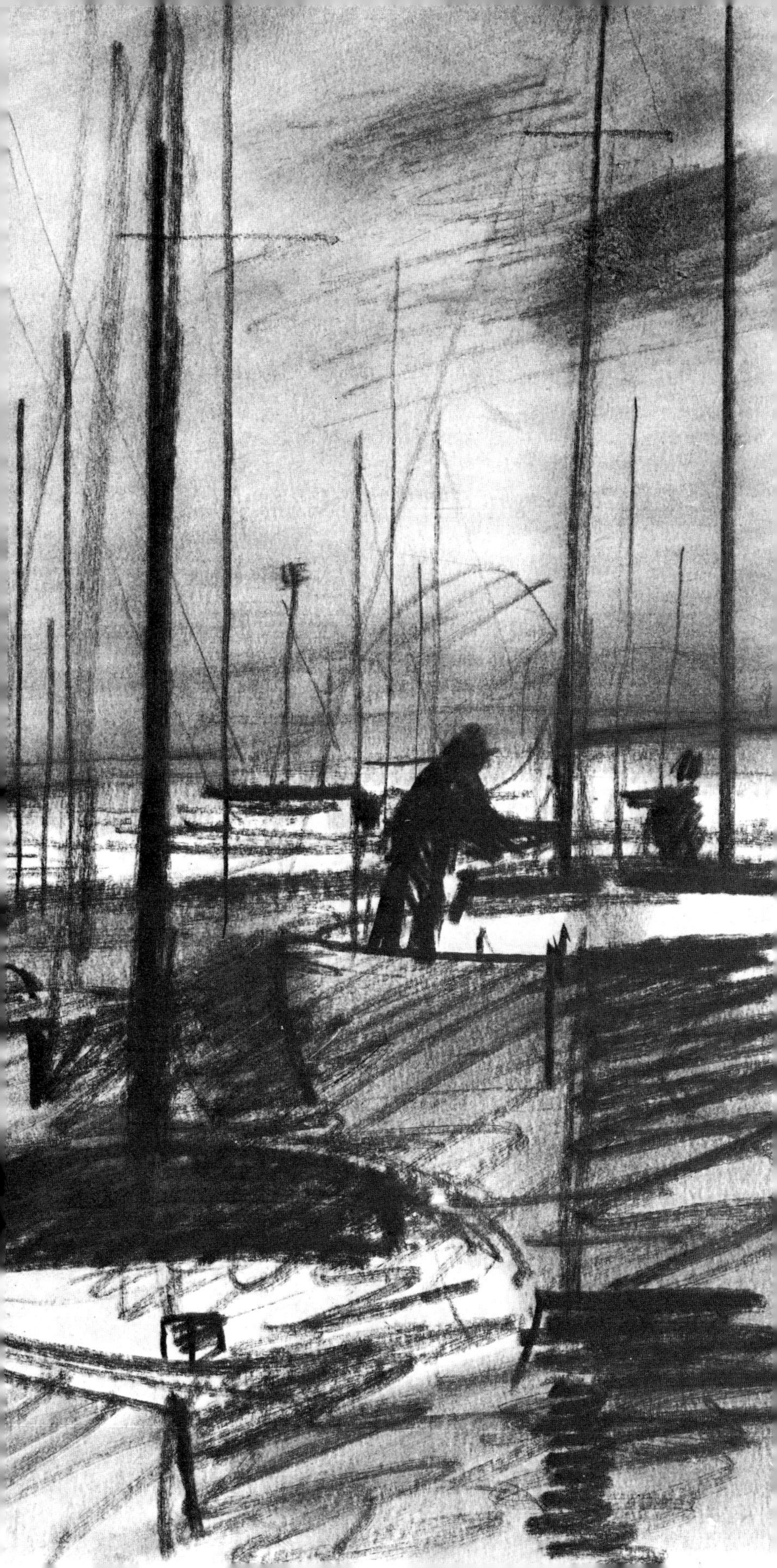

Adding tone to drawings

Most of the time drawings are thought of as being essentially linear in quality, but the use of charcoal in particular can add a remarkable amount of tone to any sketch.

Tone is the shadow used to create dimension and richness. It can be light or dark, and different intensities create very different pictures.

In the sketch of boats at night, on the previous page, I used charcoal to give a feeling of darkness and night to the picture, but in the one opposite of a riverside walk, I used charcoal to create three tones: dark for the edges of the lawn running into the water; medium for the bulk of trees and their trunks, and just the lightest touch for the reflections in the water and the masts of the boats. The white space left for the sky makes its own contribution to the scene.

Working with charcoal is a vital part of any artistic vocabulary. It is the richest black in drawing tools, yet the thin charcoal sticks can be used for very fine outlines and for adding light shadows that are far more delicate than those in a pencil drawing.

You can also use charcoal to add depth and dimension to other mediums. Try adding a little charcoal shadowing to pencil and ink outlines.

Remember that charcoal is very flaky and will need protecting as soon as your sketch is finished. Fixative comes in handy aerosols, which are much easier to control outdoors than diffusers which tend to spray everywhere except onto the picture. Do make sure the air is still before you spray, or you could cover everything in your box with a thin, sticky film.

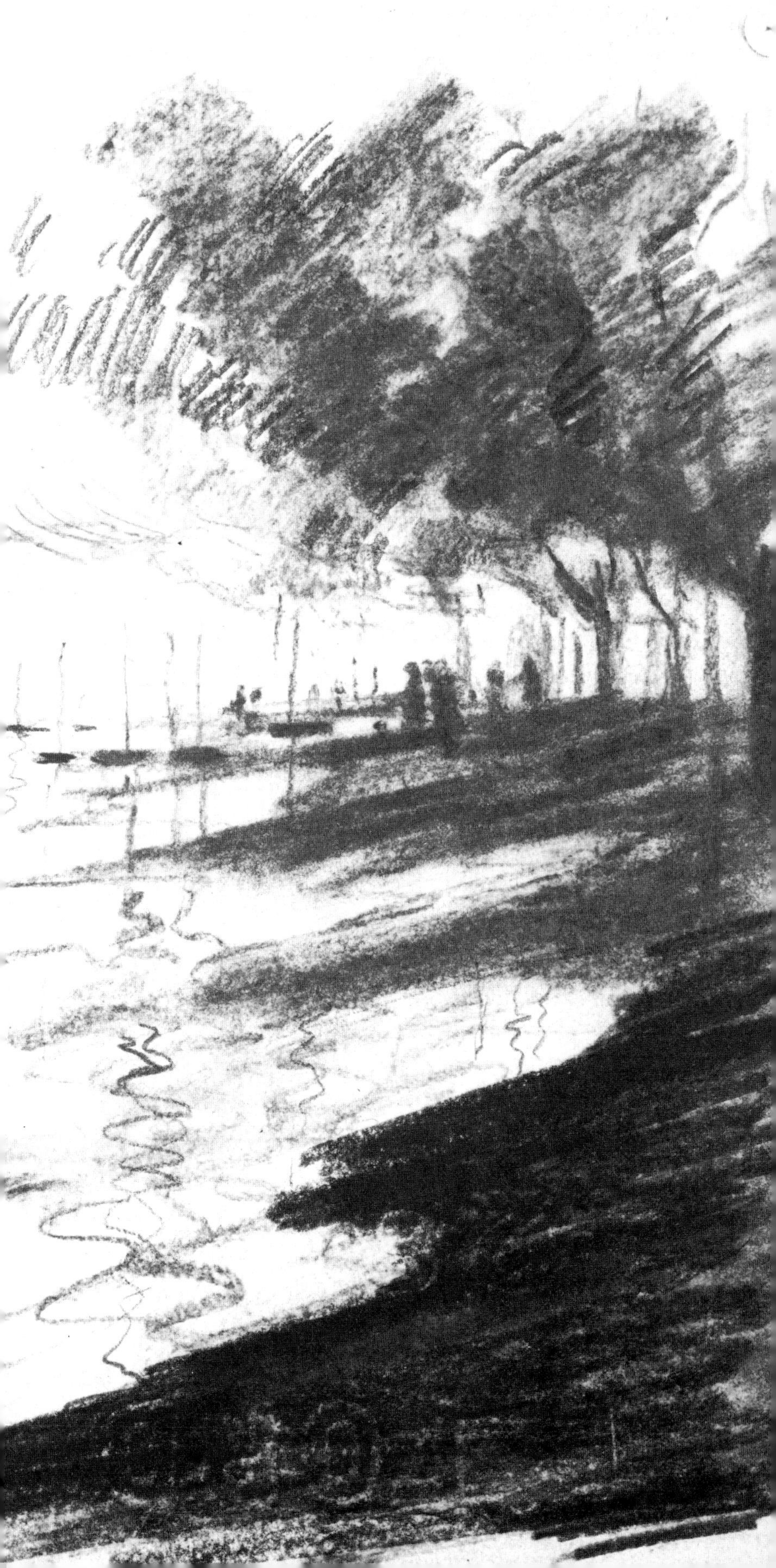

Skies

Even when you are working in black and white, cloud formations can be indicated with billowing lines, hatching can be added to darken some areas and parallel lines are an obvious, yet still effective, way of indicating rain (see the rainy scenes on page 13). Snow can be shown with flecks of grey in a softer pattern. However, when you use pastels the skies become full of colour and atmosphere.

Pale blue can be used in all its many tones for a variety of sky colours, but I also use a great deal of grey and turquoise. Because pastels are seldom precise tools for copying nature, it makes sense to give the impression of the sky colour rather than trying fruitlessly to produce the exact shade.

It is important to keep your strokes neatly parallel (top right) or you may create a messy impression with marks going off in all directions. In this sense pastels are quite different from watercolours and more like oils: brush marks in oil should not circle around the clouds. You can indicate clouds in two ways: leave white spaces; or add white pastel over the basic background (which never looks as fluffy or as white (centre right) – pastels have little covering power). I usually content myself with colouring in part of the sky and leaving spaces for the clouds, except when they are in a darker tone (bottom right).

Colour codes

In the watercolour and oil hand books, the colour codes are based on the problems and techniques of mixing pigments with each other to achieve different colours. Another approach is required with pastels, chalks and charcoal.

The examples of line and tone work in the book should extend your range with pencils and charcoal. Drawing and sketching with pastels, however, opens up a new concept of blending colours – by placing them next to each other rather than by mixing them on your palette.

Although you can buy pastels in literally hundreds of shades, if you wanted to have them all at your disposal you would have to carry hundreds of boxes with you every time you went out to sketch. It is perfectly true that your seven basic colours will not blend into each other without rubbing, but learning to use a few toning colours like greys and soft blues gives you a remarkable range of shadings. Even a simple, apparently dull, colour like grey can be brownish or yellowish, tinged with blue or purple, warm in tone or cold, and it is useful to make up colour codes with a variety of pastels, adding small or large amounts of other colours to create an entirely new palette.

Completely blend different colours by rubbing with a circular motion. Try not to rub the paper – you want to blend just the surface colour not the fibres underneath. There will always be a slight texture as flakes of pastel are caught in the tooth of the rough paper most artists use. However, if you really want the porcelain-finish of absolutely smooth colour and even tone, use a fine-surfaced paper; you will have to fix the drawing quickly. The following pages show clearly how many tones and shades can be achieved by blending pastel sticks. I have concentrated on showing how most of my favourite landscape colours react to blending with yellows, greys, greens and blues. I have included examples illustrating the variety that can be achieved with black and white, first in pastel, then in charcoal sticks from thin willow twigs to broad blocks.

Finally, a great deal of fun and pleasure can be had with felt-tip pens and coloured inks. Felt tips are useful tools, too good to be left in children's pencil boxes, while inks are widely distributed in painter's colourings. Ink washes are a convenient adaptation of one of the techniques of watercolour. They can be mixed easily, but if you are really going to experiment with subtle blends and more interesting colours for washes, instead of line work, it makes more sense to use watercolour.

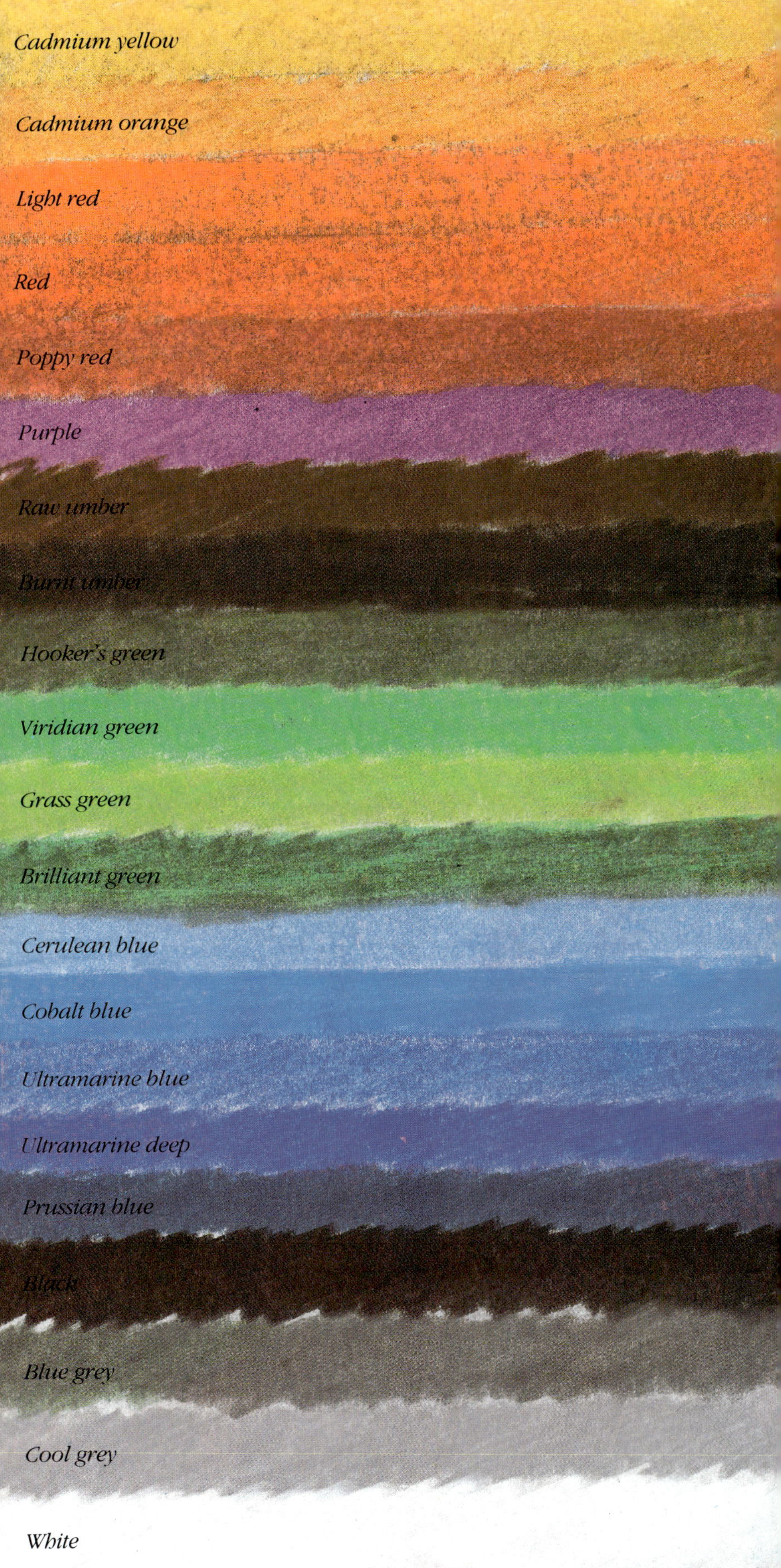

Cadmium yellow
Cadmium orange
Light red
Red
Poppy red
Purple
Raw umber
Burnt umber
Hooker's green
Viridian green
Grass green
Brilliant green
Cerulean blue
Cobalt blue
Ultramarine blue
Ultramarine deep
Prussian blue
Black
Blue grey
Cool grey
White

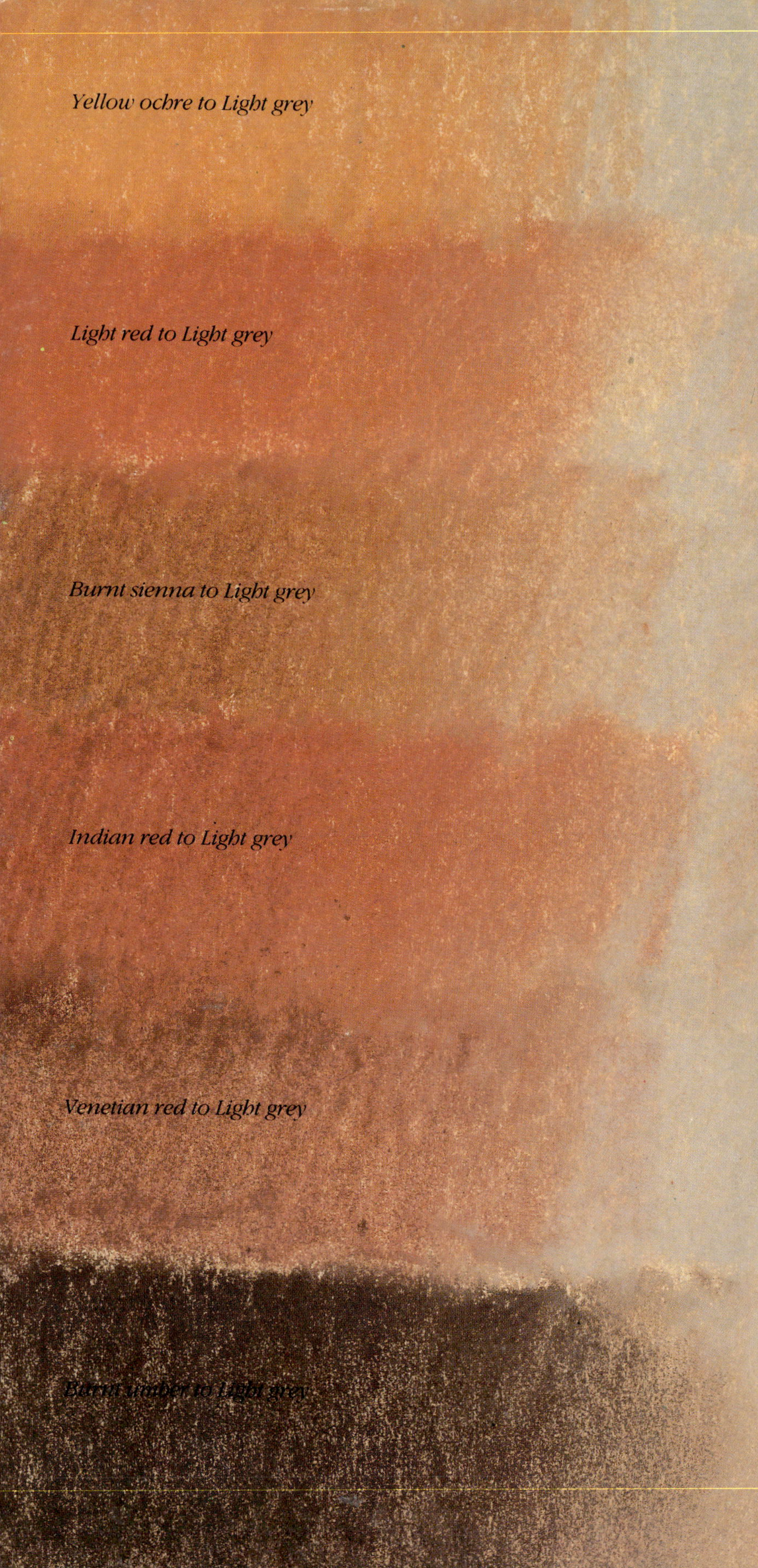
Yellow ochre to Light grey
Light red to Light grey
Burnt sienna to Light grey
Indian red to Light grey
Venetian red to Light grey
Burnt umber to Light grey

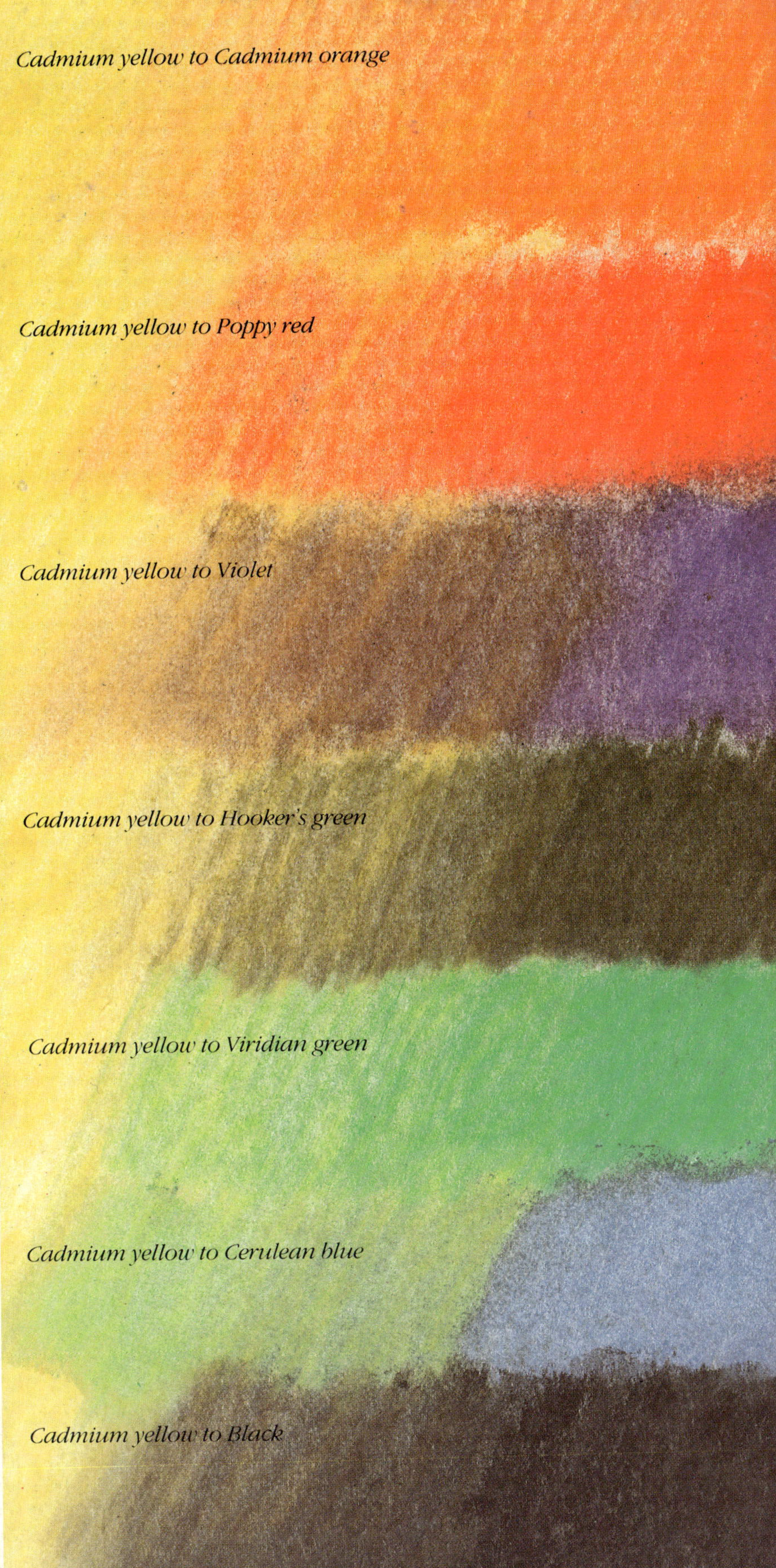

Cadmium yellow to Cadmium orange
Cadmium yellow to Poppy red
Cadmium yellow to Violet
Cadmium yellow to Hooker's green
Cadmium yellow to Viridian green
Cadmium yellow to Cerulean blue
Cadmium yellow to Black

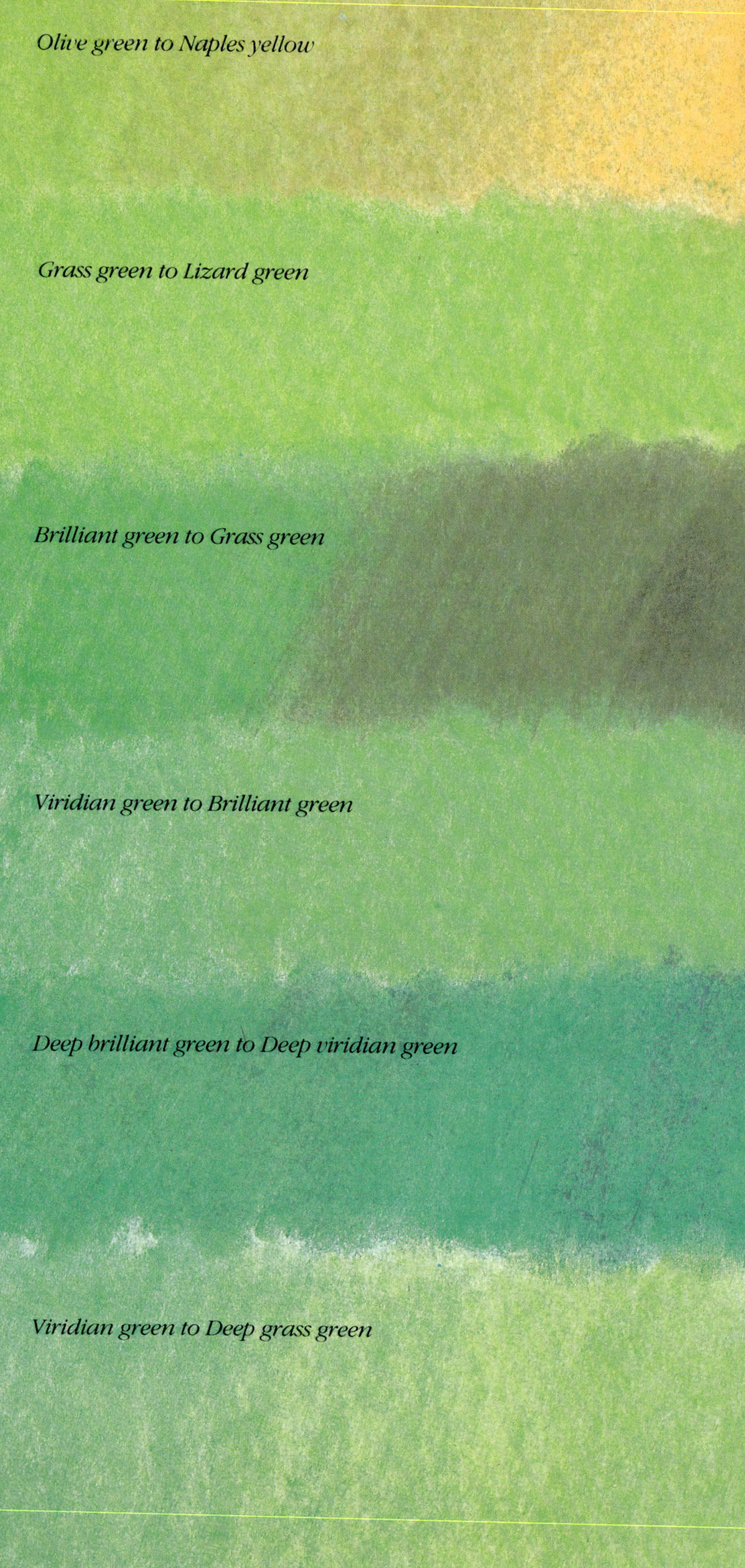
Olive green to Naples yellow
Grass green to Lizard green
Brilliant green to Grass green
Viridian green to Brilliant green
Deep brilliant green to Deep viridian green
Viridian green to Deep grass green

Mid ultramarine blue to Cadmium yellow

Mid ultramarine blue to Cadmium orange

Mid ultramarine blue to Poppy red

Mid ultramarine blue to Violet

Mid ultramarine blue to Viridian green

Mid ultramarine blue to Burnt umber

Mid ultramarine blue to Black

Lamp black to White

Deep blue grey to White

Light blue grey to White

Cool grey to White

Ivory black to Cool grey

Ivory black to Purple grey

Ivory black to Dark purple grey

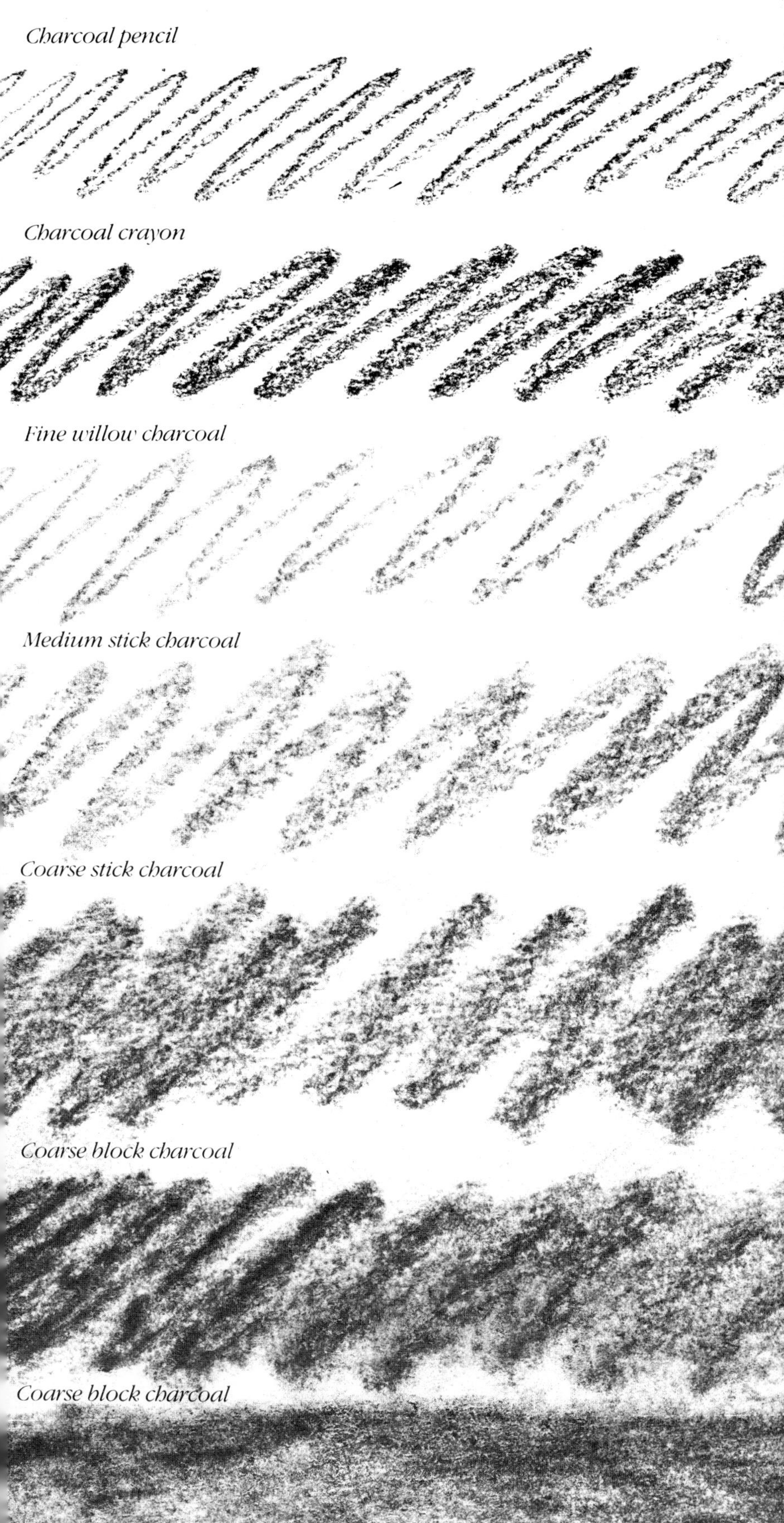
Charcoal pencil
Charcoal crayon
Fine willow charcoal
Medium stick charcoal
Coarse stick charcoal
Coarse block charcoal
Coarse block charcoal

Below are some of the most widely-distributed felt-tip colours. Like the inks, they can be blended into more subtle shades, but their fundamental appeal is that they provide quick, easy linear colour. If you want to work with greater variety and more subtlety, traditional oil or watercolour paints are still the most suitable.

Spirit-based pens are waterproof as soon as they dry, but water-based pens are not. However, you can use them like concentrated watercolour paint – especially effective when you draw directly onto wet paper.

Coloured inks in bright colours are relatively new. The colour chart opposite shows pure yellow, vermilion, carmine, scarlet, cerise, Viridian green, Cobalt blue and Ultramarine blue watered down from the pure ink through 80%, 60%, 40% and 20%, so that a line drawing can be any shade, for example from the palest pink to pure cerise.

The pure colours can be mixed for washes, but if you are going to carry a number of bottles with you, you would be better off with tubes or pans of watercolour pigments which have a much wider and more subtle range.

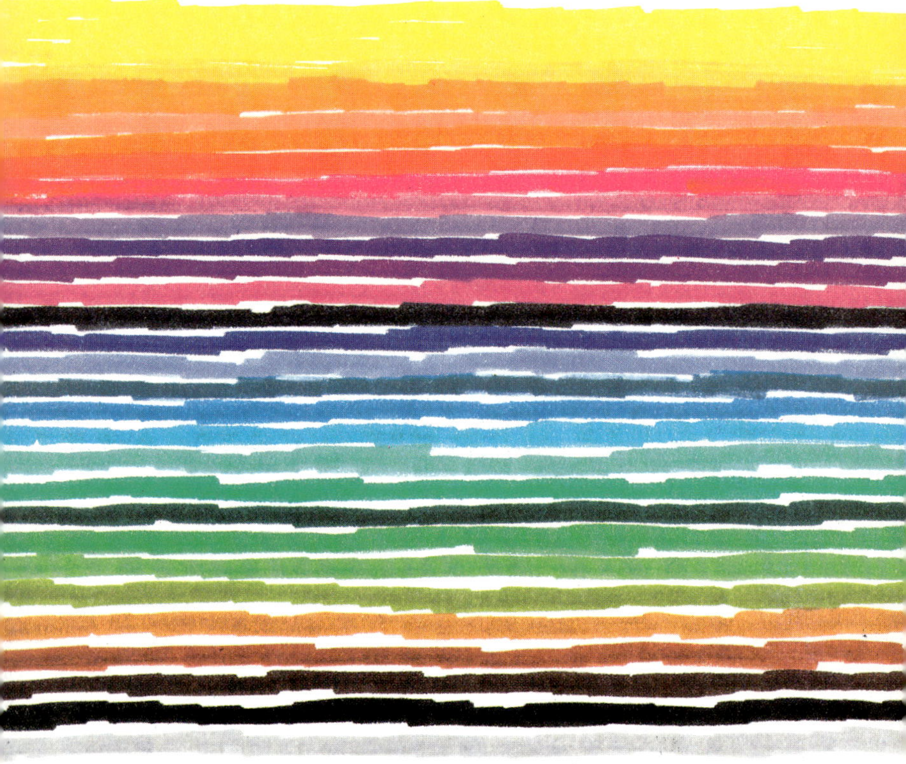

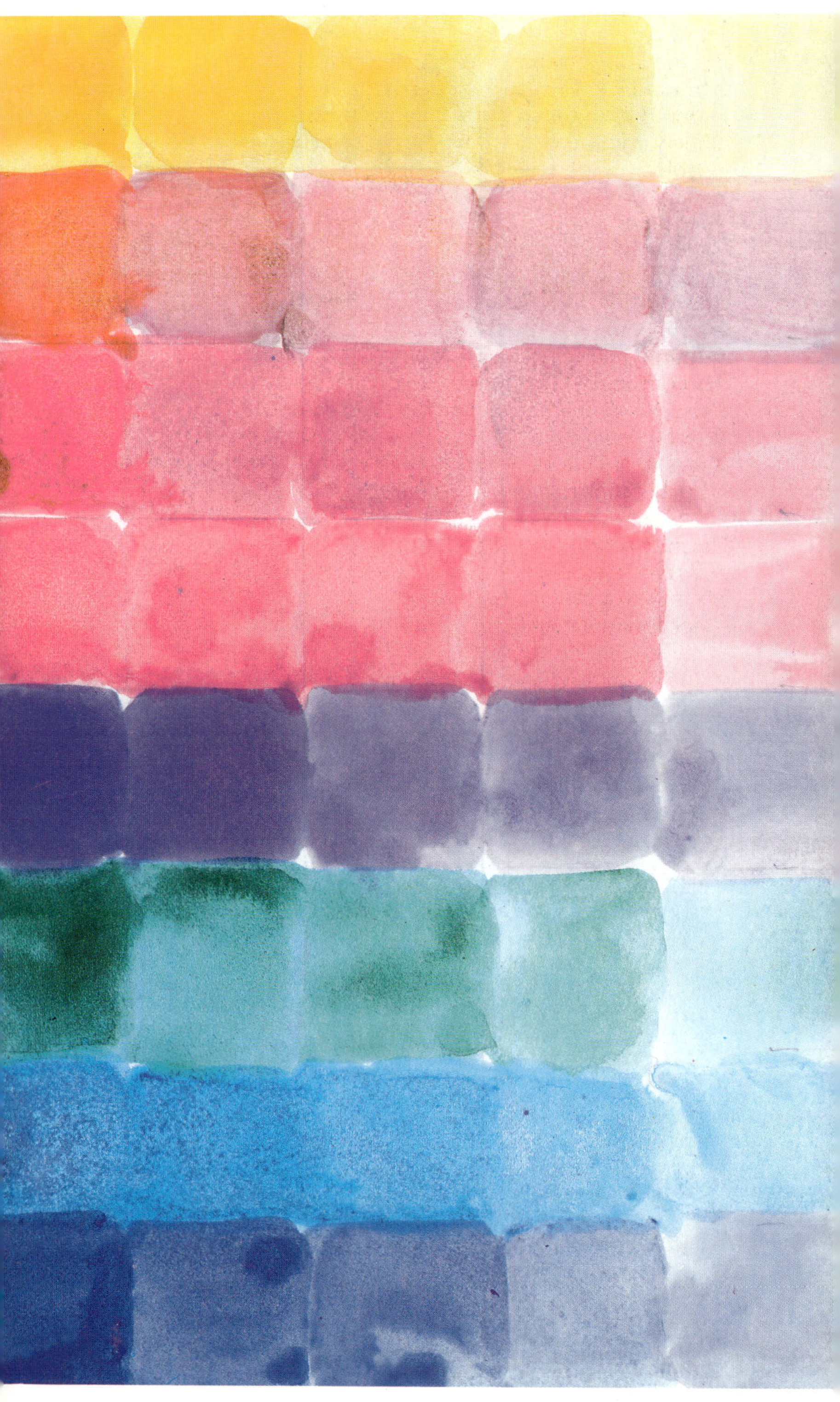

Packing up to go home

Even though a sketch pad is far easier to pack away than watercolour papers or oil canvases, there are still many small jobs to do before you are ready to leave.

As you do them, think about what you wanted to achieve and assess whether or not you have succeeded. This is an important part of the process of becoming an artist.

Look at the work you have done and ask yourself some questions.

What did I set out to do? A finished pastel sketch? A charcoal drawing? A study for a larger painting, with colour notes?

If I have completed the actual work, do I feel that the result is successful? Does the pastel colouring say what I wanted to say about the sense of air in the sky, the effect of the sun on a red dress, the moody, misty purple-blue in the distance?

Is there, above all, a feeling of space in the picture, the three-dimensional effect that, in a drawing, depends so much on the line and shape of objects in the landscape?

If not, can I pinpoint why? Perhaps the building doesn't recede enough, the angle on the street is wrong, or the doorway is too flat.

Often the tonal charcoal sketches seem more substantial than the drawings. How can I blend the two more tightly to give a better feeling of progression?

Meanwhile you should be spraying fixative both on charcoal drawings and on pastels. Although in theory oil pastels don't need fixing, they won't be harmed, and it adds an extra layer of protection. Pencil drawings must be carefully stacked together. Check ink washes to make sure that they are dry.

Pens and nibs must be cleaned and put back into their box, and pencils held together with a rubber band. Retrieve your rubber from one of the many places where it is likely to have dropped,

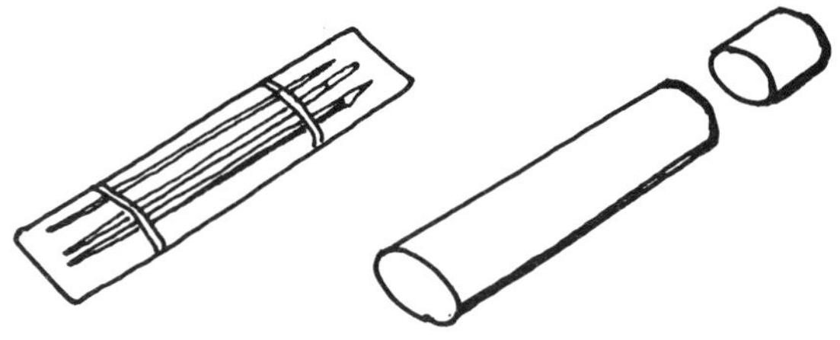

and make sure all ink bottles are tightly capped and tucked into the box.

Find your sharpening knife – it's probably in a pocket – and clean it before adding it, too, to the box. Good knives are not only expensive, but your hand gets used to holding a particular handle, and to keeping the blade at the correct angle. A new knife is always difficult to use for the first few weeks – I always spoil a few pencils while learning to deal with one if I leave my old knife behind.

When you finally set off for home, you will feel an enormous sense of satisfaction, a pleasure that comes from the knowledge that good, bad, or indifferent, the work you carry is a unique expression of your contribution to the world within the drawings.

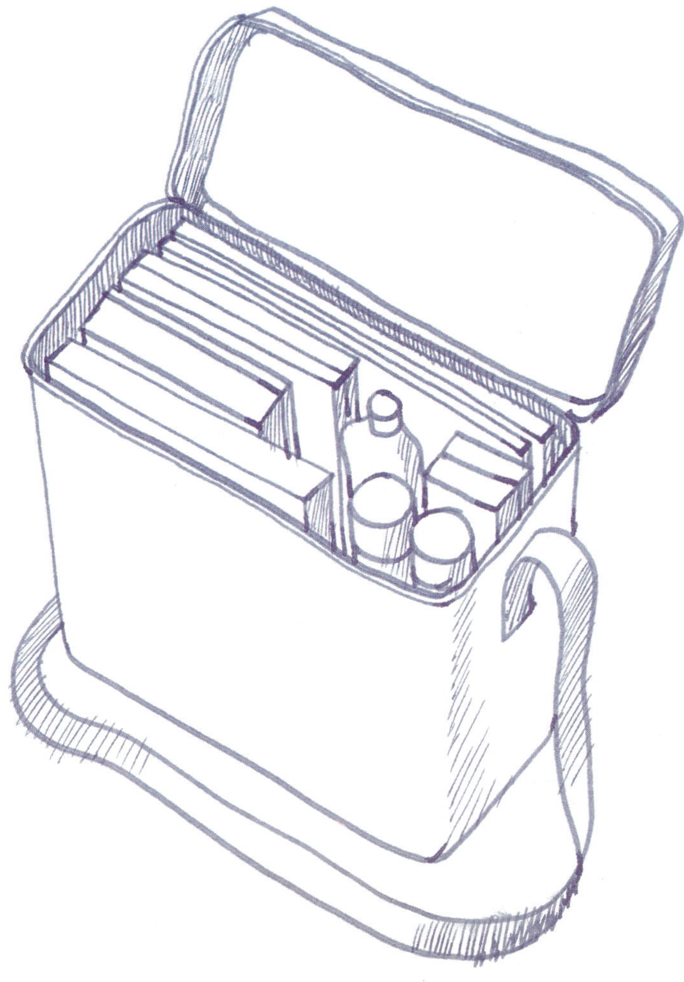

The artist's microscope

In spite of all the wonders of photography, detailed drawings are still somehow more vivid, and seem even more real, than close-up shots on colour film.

Perhaps that is because a drawing is seen through the human eye rather than through a mechanical instrument. Without being aware of it, we modify and adapt selectively when we sketch, to match our mental picture – something the camera cannot do.

Such enlightened observation is a fantastic tool in the hands of an artist, and to practise that kind of precision you must make the effort to find both time and place in which to explore, as completely as you can, a small and distinctive world.

This is particularly important if you enjoy painting landscapes as I do. Looking at the broad outline, the wide angle, the open sky, can have the effect of blurring the closer view; working on a completely different scale is wonderful training for the mind as well as the hand.

I suggest that you find somewhere out of doors that will be comfortable for as long as several weeks or even months: a local park; an empty building site; a churchyard; part of a village green; a corner of a cultivated field.

You need about twenty square feet of space, no more. If you can't get any further than your garden, try to find a spot that you don't often see or sit in, so that you will be able to look at things with an objective eye.

Start by making a rough plan on graph paper, and marking down any large features like a tree or a bench. Then pinpoint on your plan at least six or eight places that will eventually give you a more or less complete picture of your plot.

You can work round the perimeter looking inwards, or sit in the middle turning slowly round the compass. That can be interesting because of changes in lighting and different angles on objects, but you'll have to mark where your lines of comfortable vision fall, or you'll find it difficult to remember exactly which way you were facing the last time you started to work.

Once having marked out your viewing plan, sit down at your easel and draw everything you can see within a comfortable front focus, and as far as the edge of your plan.

Make sure you include the texture of stones, weeds, dead leaves, clumps of dandelions – whatever there is within that space. Work carefully, thinking about what you put down.

Do the same view in charcoal, in pencil and in pastels.

Make another sketch in ink wash and pen line.

If you cannot see the detail of a plant, get closer with a pad, draw in the fine points and transfer this to the main drawing. Take all the time you need.

Plan to be in the same place at the same time for your next session, and go on until every square foot has been mapped, drawn and sketched.

At the end of the project, you will have a most valuable record of the area's ecology, and an equally valuable record for yourself of what can be achieved with patience, time and concentration.

Your observation will have been sharpened to a remarkable degree, and you should find yourself able to draw quickly with more fluency and confidence than at the start.

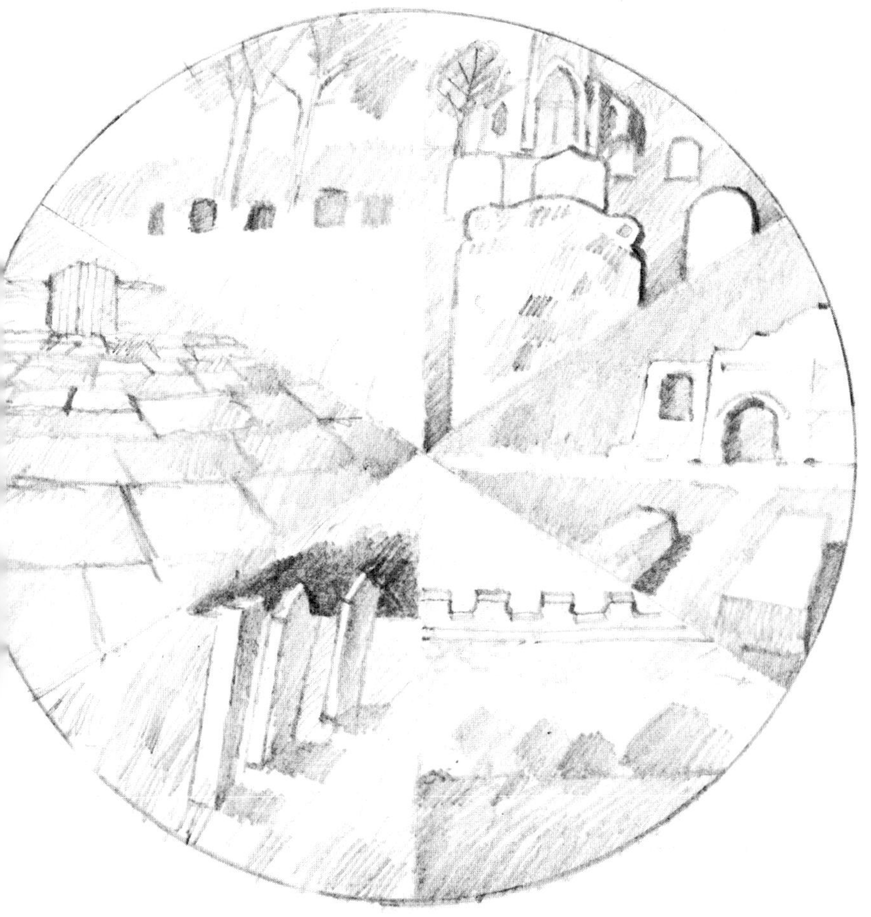

Index

Page numbers in *italic* refer to and illustrations.

Note on colour charts: the guides in this book have been produced within the limitations of four-colour process printing, and therefore cannot reflect the intensity of certain pure pigments.